JEWISH
CONTEMPORARIES
OF JESUS

JEWISH CONTEMPORARIES OF JESUS

PHARISEES, SADDUCEES, ESSENES

GÜNTER STEMBERGER

TRANSLATED BY ALLAN W. MAHNKE

FORTRESS PRESS

MINNEAPOLIS

JEWISH CONTEMPORARIES OF JESUS
Pharisees, Sadducees, Essenes

First published in English by Fortress Press, 1995
English translation copyright © 1995 Augsburg Fortress

Translated from *Pharisäer, Sadduzäer, Essener* © 1991 Verlag Katholisches Bibelwerk
GmbH, Stuttgart. Gesamtherstellung: Wilhelm Röck GmbH, Weinsberg.

Quotations from the Apocrypha from the *Revised English Bible* are copyright © 1989 by the
Oxford and Cambridge University Presses. Used by permission. Scripture quotations from
the New Revised Standard Version of the Bible are copyright © 1989 by the Division of
Christian Education of the National Council of Churches of Christ in the USA and are used
by permission.

Cover design: David Meyer
Interior layout: David Lott
Cover art: Josephus with oversized Jews' hat. Miniature, 12th Cent. Latin ms. of *Antiquities.*

Library of Congress Cataloging-in-Publication data

Stemberger, Günter, 1940–
    [Pharisäer, Sadduzäer, Essener. English]
    Jewish contemporaries of Jesus / Gunter Stemberger ; Allan W.
Mahnke, translator.
        p.   cm.
    Includes bibliographical references and index.
    ISBN 0-8006-2624-9 (alk. paper)
    1. Pharisees. 2. Sadducees. 3. Essenes. 4. Judaism—History—
Post-exilic period, 586 B.C.–210 A.D.   I. Title.
BM175.P4S7413   1995
296.8′ 1—dc20   95-37196
                                                          CIP

The paper used in this publication meets the minimum requirements of American National
Standard for Information Sciences—Permanence of Paper for Printed Library Materials,
ANSI Z329.48-1984.

Manufactured in the U.S.A.   AF 1-2624

06   05   04   03   02   01   00   2   3   4   5   6   7   8

CONTENTS

Abbreviations and References

1. Mishnah, Tosepta, Talmudim

The abbreviations for the tractates of these works are always the same. To distinguish the references, the Mishnah is cited according to chapter and *halakah* and preceded by *m.* (e.g., *m. Hag.* 2.1), the Babylonian Talmud according to sheet and side a or b and preceded by *b.* (e.g., *b. Yoma* 53a); references from the Jersualem Talmud are preceded by *y.* (e.g., *y. RošHaš.* 2.1.57d, indicating chapter, *halakah*, page, and column); those from the Tosepta are preceded by *t.* (e.g., *t. Hag. 3.25,* followed by an abbreviation of the critical edition: Lieberman = S. Lieberman, *Tosefta* [New York, 1955ff.]; Rengstorf = K. H. Rengstorf, ed., *Die Tosefta* [Stuttgart, 1960ff.]; where the critical edition is not yet available: Zuckermandel = M. Zuckermandel, *Tosephta* [Pasewalk, 1880; repr. Jerusalem, 1963].

B. Bat.	Baba Batra
Bek.	Bekorot
Ber.	Berakot
ʿErub.	ʿErubin
Ḥag.	Ḥagiga
Hor.	Horayot
Ḥul.	Ḥullin
Mak.	Makkot
Meg.	Megilla
Menaḥ.	Menaḥot
Nid.	Niddah
Pesaḥ.	Pesaḥim
Qidd.	Qiddusin

Roš Haš.	Roš Haššana
Sanh.	Sanhedrin
Šabb.	Šabbat
Sukk.	Sukka
Yad.	Yadayim

2. Hellenistic Jewish, Pseudepigraphical, and Early Patristic Books

AJ	Josephus, *Antiquities of the Jews*
BJ	Josephus, *Bellum Judaicum (Jewish War)*
H.E.	Eusebius, *Historica Ecclesiastica (History of the Church)*
Spec. leg.	Philo, *De specialibus legibus*

3. Dead Sea Scrolls and Related Texts

CD	Cairo (Genizah) text of the *Damascus Document*
1QS	*Serek hayyaḥad (Rule of the Community, [Manual of Discipline])*
1QSa	Appendix A *(Rule of the Congregation)* to 1QS
1QpHab	*Pešer on Habbakuk* from Qumran Cave 1
4QpHos^b	*Pešer on Hosea* from Qumran Cave 4
4QpNah	*Pešer on Nahum* from Qumran Cave 4
4QpPs^a	*Pešer on Psalms* from Qumran Cave 4
4QTest	*Testimonia* from Qumran Cave 4
11QT	*Temple Scroll* from Qumran Cave 11

4. Other Texts

ʾAbot R. Nat.	ʾAbot de Rabbi Nathan, text A or B; Schechter = S. Schechter edition (Vienna, 1887; repr. New York, 1967).
LevR	*Leviticus Rabbah;* Marguilies = M. Marguilies, *Midrash Wayyikra Rabbah,* 5 vols. (Jerusalem, 1953–60).
Mek.	*Mekhilta;* Lauterbach = J. Z. Lauterbach, *Mekilta de Rabbi Ishmael,* 3 vols. (Heb.-Eng.) (Philadelphia, 1933–35).
Sifra	Weiss = I. H. Weiss, *Sifra debei rabh* (Vienna, 1862).

Sifre Num	*Sifre zu Numeri;* Horowitz = H. S. Horowitz, *Siphre D'be Rab: Fasciculus primus: Siphre ad Numeros adjecto Siphre zutta,* 2d ed. (Jerusalem, 1966).

5. Journals, Reference Works, and Serials

AB	Anchor Bible
ANRW	*Aufsteig und Niedergang der römischen Welt*
Bib	*Biblica*
BZ	*Biblische Zeitschrift*
DJD	*Discoveries in the Judaean Desert*
HTR	*Harvard Theological Review*
HUCA	*Hebrew Union College Annual*
JANESCU	*Journal of the Near Eastern Society of Columbia University*
JBL	*Journal of Biblical Literature*
JJS	*Journal of Jewish Studies*
JQR	*Jewish Quarterly Review*
JSHRZ	Jüdische Schriften aus hellenistisch-römischen Zeit
JSJ	*Journal for the Study of Judaism in the Persian, Hellenistic, and Roman Period*
NovT	*Novum Testamentum*
NTS	*New Testament Studies*
RB	*Revue biblique*
REJ	*Revue des études juives*
RQ	*Römische Quartalschrift für christliche Altertumskunde und Kirchengeschichte*
SR	*Studies in Religion/Sciences religeuses*
TWNT	G. Kittel and G. Friedrich, eds., *Theologisches Wörterbuch zum Neuen Testament*
VT	*Vetus Testamentum*
ZNW	*Zeitschrift für die neutestamentliche Wissenschaft*
ZRGG	*Zeitschrift für Religions- und Geistesgeschichte*

INTRODUCTION

As is well known, any attempt to portray the religious movements
of Palestinian Judaism during the New Testament period will
encounter great difficulties. The main problem is the source
material. When we read the various descriptions of the history of
Jewish religious parties, we often forget that the designation *Pharisee* is not found before Paul, or the name *Sadducee* before Mark's
Gospel. Writing slightly later, at about the same time as the other
texts of the New Testament, was Flavius Josephus, who added the
third school of Judaism, the Essenes. This means that the earliest
explicit statements about Pharisees and Sadducees were first written
at a time when they had ceased to exist. Only the third group, the
Essenes, has been extensively documented by the Qumran texts,
although a direct equation of Qumran and the Essenes is still
disputed.

The Qumran texts take us farther back in time and are an essential source for Jewish history since the Maccabean period. Nevertheless, the increased interest in the Essenes stimulated by discoveries made during the last few decades should not obscure the
fact that they were a rather radical, marginal group. This situation is
documented by their own statements and by Josephus. Furthermore,
neither the New Testament nor rabbinic literature mentions them.
We need to explain this silence if we wish to shed light on the
relations of the Essenes to other movements of their time. The
extent of the available sources should not mislead us into exagger-
ating the importance of the Essenes in the history of that period. In
addition, there is already a vast, specialized literature for Qumran
that will allow us to discuss the Essenes only in relation to the other
groups and not as an independent force.

Josephus is the only author who goes into the history of the three groups, but how does he know about them? Nicolaus of Damascus, the court scribe of Herod, was his primary source, and we can only surmise about Josephus's other material. Anyone who tries to make a historical reconstruction tracing the Pharisees and Sadducees back into the Maccabean period or even further must have absolute confidence in Josephus and his unnamed sources and also in developmental lines connecting biblical writings with postbiblical Judaism. To be sure, much of this is legitimate, but we must be cognizant of the dangers.

We nearly always refer back to other texts when reconstructing the spiritual and political history of religious groups. Many authors try to parcel out the extant literature of the Second Temple to the Pharisees, Sadducees, and Essenes—even when those names do not appear—in order to find reference to each respective group and its rivals. Here too, much is plausible, even if hard to prove. The fundamental assumption—that all of Judaism during the approximately three hundred years from the Maccabees to the destruction of the Temple in 70 C.E. is reduceable to these three groups—is problematic. The numbers mentioned by Josephus, as problematic as they are, should serve as a warning against this. Filling out the picture with texts from Qumran, in which we might think that we find various references to Pharisees and Sadducees, is attractive and occasionally even probable; but the texts do not mention the rivals by name, which, in addition to all the other difficulties involved with historical evaluation of the Qumran texts, leaves much to speculation.

It is common knowledge and only too natural that the New Testament texts do not offer unbiased descriptions of the Pharisees and Sadducees. For that reason, with regard to both Jewish and Christian authors one usually tries to find corrective and supplementary material, at least for the Pharisees, in rabbinic texts. There are two problems with this fundamental assumption: on the one hand, there was more or less direct continuity between the Pharisees before 70 C.E. and the rabbis after the fall of Jerusalem; on the other hand, the reliability and usability of rabbinic statements for conditions in previous centuries is suspect. It is obvious that statements by rabbis about the Sadducees will hardly be objective, but even the few paragraphs by the rabbis about the Pharisees are probably to be understood as clarification of their own beginnings, to the extent that the historical Pharisees are discussed at all. We will discuss this terminology further.

We can also describe briefly another terminological problem. Usually, we speak of "religious parties" or "sects." Josephus, who originated this usage, most often employs the ambiguous expression *hairesis*, with its suggestion of heresy. But most probably it means 'different point of view, teaching, or direction of thought.' This common term, introduced for Greek and Roman readers, may be usable for characteristics of the three groups described by Josephus: for a historical description, however, there is the problem that, from this vantage point, these three groups are seen a priori as comparable entities, even if only a few features are in fact comparable. The term *party,* which may be a religious party, causes us to imagine specific organizational forms, membership, and policies. With the exception of the Essenes, there are still no sources for potential organizational forms of each group, and thus we will have to pass over this question.[1]

In general, so that our task might remain manageable, I will refer only occasionally to classic literature on the Pharisees and Sadducees, and I will limit myself largely to recent studies. For the same reason, and without ignoring the many historical problems and unanswerable questions, I will treat the Pharisees and Sadducees together in my first examination of the sources, even if in doing this I give the Sadducees short shrift. Josephus, as a text

1. For attempts to delineate the organization of the groups more closely, see, for example, J. Jeremias, *Jerusalem,* II.B.98. He regards the three groups as "closed associations with clear requirements for admission and rules" (for the Pharisees developed by comparison with the *chaburot,* for the Sadducees by simple analogy.) Somewhat more cautious is A. J. Saldarini, *Pharisees,* 122, who assumes for the Pharisees "a leadership structure, education for their members and clear criteria for membership," while the Sadducees may have been an identifiable school, yet "without having a highly articulated community structure" (123).

within Judaism, takes precedence over the New Testament passages I will discuss individually, as well as over the rabbinic writings. Of course, the New Testament is primarily polemical in nature, and the rabbinic writings are much later and equally one-sided. The second part of this book attempts a reconstruction of the spiritual profile as well as the beginnings and histories of each group. In this part I will draw on the texts from Qumran, thus far neglected, and the intertestamental literature appropriate to this context. Only then, in a shorter section, can we discuss the community of Qumran and the larger group of the Essenes and attempt a classification of the spiritual-religious relationships of that period. A closing section will treat briefly the developments after 70 C.E.

ONE

PHARISEES AND SADDUCEES: THE SOURCES

1. FLAVIUS JOSEPHUS

1.1 Josephus—A Pharisee?

Josephus is the primary source in every description of the Jewish religious parties of the first century. He is the only Pharisee known by name, other than Paul, from whom we have written evidence about this group. In addition, he is the only one who also knew and described other groups from personal experience. To be sure, after 70 C.E. he was only a marginal figure in the Jewish world; his detailed observations regarding current religious movements are, nonetheless, a most reliable report from a man who was acquainted with the relationships from the inside—at least until 70 C.E.

Josephus came from a noble family of priests, related to the Hasmoneans, so we might expect him to be a Sadducee. In his biography, written in 94 C.E. or shortly thereafter, in which he tries to justify his posture in the war against Rome, he classifies himself as a Pharisee. He wrote about his youth:

> At about the age of sixteen I determined to gain personal experience of the several sects into which our nation is divided. These, as I have frequently mentioned, are three in number—the first that of the Pharisees, the second that of the Sadducees, and the third that of the Essenes. I thought that, after a thorough investigation, I should be in a position to select the best. So I submitted myself to hard training and laborious exercises and passed through the three courses.

Not content, however, with the experience thus gained, on hearing of
one named Bannus, who dwelt in the wilderness, wearing only such
clothing as trees provided, feeding on such things as grew of themselves, and using frequent ablutions of cold water, by day and night,
for purity's sake, I became his devoted disciple. With him I lived for
three years and, having accomplished my purpose, returned to the
city. Being now in my nineteenth year I began to govern my life by
the rules of the Pharisees, a sect having points of resemblance to that
which the Greeks call the Stoic school. (*Vita* 10–12)

Let us set aside the fact that Josephus describes his youth here
completely according to the Hellenistic educational ideal of all-
encompassing development. Even if we regard the text as a factual
report, it is remarkable that Josephus, according to his own statement, would spend practically the whole time that he intended to
dedicate to an examination of the three schools of thought in contemporary Judaism in the company of the hermit Bannus. The end
of the citation is usually understood to mean that Josephus, after
prudent consideration, decided in favor of the Pharisees, and that he
joined that "party." Did he conclude, after his very brief examination, that the Pharisees were the best choice—in spite of his enthusiasm for Bannus? Why does he not say it in so many words? In
fact, there is an emphasis on the word *politeuesthai* in the last
sentence, the selection of a public career, to which the remark about
the Pharisees is subordinated as a participial phrase. In other words,
he chose a public career for which Bannus could have been of little
help. This could have been a purely pragmatic decision having
nothing to do with joining a party.[2] That means that we should not

2. This interpretation of the passage has most recently been convincingly developed by S. N. Mason, *Was Josephus a Pharisee?* See also J. Le Moyne, *Le
Sadducéens*, 29, n. 1, "Rentrant a Jérusalem, il choisit un idéal de vie, celui des
Pharisiens . . . Mais il ne s'agrége pas au groupe, et reste dans la mouvance
sadducéenne de son milieu familial." S. J. D. Cohen, *Josephus*, 144-51, noted a
shift in bias from *BJ* to *AJ* in the sense of a "religious-Pharisaic bias . . . ; his
Pharisaism is of the most dubious variety, and he did not discover it until the
nineties of our era. In the sixties he was a Jerusalem priest and, in all likelihood,
not a Pharisee" (p. 223). J. Ephron, *Studies*, 173, also misses "any genuine personal links or close connections with the Pharisees" in Josephus.

regard Josephus as definitely a member of the Pharisaic party as he is usually seen. This does not change our evaluation of his direct knowledge of the Pharisees, but it does cast a different light on many of the tensions in things he said.

1.2 The *Jewish War*

Various authors have emphasized that Josephus portrayed the Pharisees more positively in his later *Antiquities* than in the earlier *Jewish War*. This may have had a political purpose. Even if this does not affect the Sadducees and Essenes so directly, it does suggest that the total corpus of Josephus's work ought not to be regarded as a unity, but we should begin with the *Jewish War,* the Greek version of which was based on an earlier Aramaic draft and was completed in 75 and 79 C.E. The Sadducees appear here only in a synopsis of the three branches of Judaism (2.118ff.). Only the Pharisees played a historical role; Josephus mentioned them for the first time during the reign of Salome Alexandra (76–67 B.C.E.). He says that during her rule the Pharisees grew stronger and stronger:

> The Pharisees, a body of Jews with the reputation of excelling the rest of their nation in the observances of religion, and as exact exponents of the laws. To them, being herself intensely religious, she listened with too great deference; while they, gradually taking advantage of an ingenuous woman, became at length the real administrators of the state, at liberty to banish and to recall, to loose and to bind, whom they would. In short, the enjoyments of royal authority were theirs; its expenses and burthens fell to Alexandra. She proved, however, to be a wonderful administrator in larger affairs, and, by continual recruiting doubled her army, besides collecting a considerable body of foreign troops; so that she not only strengthened her own nation, but became a formidable foe to foreign potentates. But if she ruled the nation, the Pharisees ruled her. (*BJ* 1.110–12)

The Pharisees executed Diogenes because he advised Alexander Jannai to crucify 800 of his opponents (1.97: they were not yet called Pharisees here), and they urged Alexandra to punish other people. "Since she was superstitious, they executed whomever they wanted," but many fled to Aristobolus (1.113f.).

This is hardly a positive first chapter of a description of the Pharisees, certainly not a sympathetic portrayal by a member of the movement. His positive statements (more pious and stricter observance of the law) are diluted to subjective evaluation (*dokoun*: "They have the reputation"). The narrator's sympathy is with Alexandra, to whom he pays tribute in 1.112. It was only because of her exaggerated piety, her superstition, that she was entrapped by the Pharisees, who used her in a campaign of revenge. Because of the negative attitude of this text toward the Pharisees, some people have thought it was the work of one of their enemies, Nicolaus of Damascus, the pagan historian in the court of Herod.[3] If that is the case, why did Josephus not revise the account accordingly?

The next mention of the Pharisees occurs at the beginning of Herod's reign. He accused his brother Pheroras's wife of, among other things, "raising money against the Pharisees" (1.571; we learn more from the later parallel *AJ* 17.42).[4] Josephus gave his only systematic portrayal of the schools of thought in Judaism in connection with the transformation of Archelaus's territory into a Roman province in 6 C.E. At that time, the Galilean Judas appeared, "an itinerant preacher of some school (*sophistēs idias haireseōs*)," completely different from the others (*BJ* 2.118). That motivated Josephus to write an excursus on the three philosophical schools of the Jews: the Pharisees, the Sadducees, and the Essenes (119–66). The Essenes alone he treated thoroughly. He characterized by contrasts the Pharisees and the Sadducees only in his conclusion. As in 1.110, he said of the Pharisees, "They are said to observe the law with precision and are the first [most prominent or earliest?] school." He described the Pharisaic concepts of fate and afterlife, contrasting them with the Sadducees (see the following chapter), and then continued:

> The Pharisees are affectionate to each other and cultivate harmonious relations with the community. The Sadducees, on the contrary,

---

3. See D. R. Schwartz, *Josephus and Nicolaus,* 120.
4. E. Rivkin, *A Hidden Revolution.* He treats *BJ* and *AJ* generally as saying the same thing. He apparently overlooks this spot in *BJ*. See the parallel in *AJ* 17 for his treatment of that passage.

are, even among themselves, rather boorish in their behaviour, and in their intercourse with their peers are as rude as to aliens. Such is what I have to say on the Jewish philosophical schools. (*BJ* 2.166)

This is probably not just a description of the solidarity of the Pharisaic community, but also of their attitude toward Jewish society. The portrayal of the Sadducees that follows mentions the relationship to their own people and to the other Jews (that is more probable as a contrast of Jews and non-Jews).

There is no more discussion of the Sadducees in this work. The only other mention of the Pharisees occurs at the beginning of the uprising against Rome: "The powerful gathered with the high priests and the best-known Pharisees" (2.411), in order—unsuccessfully—to negotiate with the members of the insurrection for a peaceful stance, faithful to Rome. This is the only place where Josephus has written from personal knowledge (in which, however, his own vested interest with respect to Roman readers could have played a part).

Had we only this reference, we would know only that the Sadducees were a Jewish school, characterized by thinking that differed in a few points from the Pharisees and especially that they were, to a degree, uncooperative. To Josephus, whether this intransigence was out of principle or general lack of social skills made no difference; he had little sympathy for the Sadducees.

Where they appeared, the Pharisees were described in an extremely negative manner. They proved to be vengeful under Salome Alexandra, whose faith and piety they misused. And under Herod they plotted intrigues with the women of his family. When the great insurrection occurred, their leaders pleaded, rather astonishingly, with the leaders of the people for peace with Rome, but they did not have enough influence to be successful. The systematic descriptions of the Pharisees in 2.162ff. and 1.110, by contrast, sound positive: they are the first school and have a reputation for piety and knowledge of the law (but the author does not guarantee this!); they stayed together and worked for harmony among the people. This does not quite fit with the historical description. In general, the historical picture has many gaps, and the relationship between religious point of view and political conduct is quite unclear. Dependence upon Nicolaus of Damascus does not alone account for the thoroughly negative description of the Pharisees; Josephus is apparently in agreement.

1.3 The *Jewish Antiquities*

The *Jewish Antiquities*, completed between 93 and 94, adds a series of additional bits of information. The three schools are mentioned here for the first time in 13.171-73, in the midst of a retelling of 1 Maccabees 12, in the time of the high priest Jonathan (161–143 B.C.E.). Josephus also expressly refers to a summary of *BJ* 2.119ff. In this context he mentions only the concepts of fate held by each group. In this connection Josephus notes the jealousy that the military successes of John Hyrcanus aroused in the people (but why?[5]). He added here the story of the break between Hyrcanus and the Pharisees. I will go into the historical question later, but here I am interested in the characterization of the Pharisees and Sadducees.

> As for Hyrcanus, the envy of the Jews was aroused against him by his own successes and those of his sons; particularly hostile to him were the Pharisees, who are one of the Jewish schools, as we have related above. And so great is their influence with the masses that even when they speak against a king or high priest, they immediately gain credence. Hyrcanus too was a disciple of theirs, and was greatly loved by them. (*AJ* 13.288f.)

The description of the Pharisees is double-faceted. The introduction speaks of their negative posture toward John Hyrcanus and the dangerous political influence they had over the population, which was so great that they could even agitate against the king or the

---

5. J. Efron, *Studies*, 161, refers to *BJ* 1.208, where it says of the young Herod's ascent to the throne, "But it is impossible to escape the jealousy of the people through success." Nicolaus of Damascus, the basis of the portrait of Herod in Josephus, may also be the source for the description of the Hasmoneans. This would explain the negative picture of the Jewish people, especially the Pharisees.

high priest.[6] Still, the continuation shows that they had no cause, since they otherwise favored Hyrcanus, and he was on their side. Then there is a story telling how Hyrcanus invited the Pharisees to a banquet and said to them that he wanted to be upright, pleasing God and the Pharisees in all things. If he had done something wrong, they should correct him. Everyone praised him except Eleazar, "who had a bad character and was quarrelsome" (290). He demanded that Hyrcanus give up his office as high priest because, according to the rumor, his mother was a prisoner of war, and thus his lineage was not beyond reproach. The Pharisees distanced themselves from this slander, but a Sadducee with whom Hyrcanus had a close friendship convinced him that this, in reality, was what the Pharisees generally believed to be the actual state of affairs. As a proof, the Sadducee suggested that the Pharisees ought to have punished Eleazar for the slander. Because they were gentle people by nature, they pleaded for whip and chains instead of the death penalty. But Hyrcanus regarded the opinion of the Sadducee as correct, so he quit the Pharisees, nullified the laws they had passed, and became a Sadducee.

The break between the introduction and the narrative makes it clear that Josephus combined material from different sources that had different attitudes toward the Pharisees. At the outset, they were dangerous opponents of Hyrcanus (288); his break with them caused Hyrcanus and his sons to be hated by the people. In contrast, the story that was inserted describes the friendly relationship between Hyrcanus and the Pharisees, which was destroyed by a characterless member who exploited the situation in a cold-blooded fashion. The Pharisees were innocent, and even Hyrcanus was only misled. The Sadducees, on the other hand, who were only described in contrast to the Pharisees ("who represented the opposite point of

---

6. D. R. Schwartz, *Josephus and Nicolaus,* 158, correctly emphasizes that this formulation is more appropriate to the time of Herod, and he sees Nicolaus of Damascus behind the hostile statements about the Pharisees. We might even find him behind the parallel *BJ* 1.67f. In that passage Josephus must simply have omitted the Pharisees.

view of the Pharisees," 293), are presented without their own profile and in a completely negative fashion.

Additionally, Josephus comments on the story with a reference to statements from the patriarchal tradition, which the Pharisees accepted—while the Sadducees were satisfied only with the written laws. This led to significant differences between the two groups:

> . . . the Sadducees having the confidence of the wealthy alone but no following among the populace, while the Pharisees have the support of the masses. (*AJ* 13.298f.)

The next time the Pharisees appear is in the death scene of Alexander Jannai, who advised his wife:

> She should yield a certain amount of power to the Pharisees, for if they praised her in return for this sign of regard, they would dispose the nation favourably toward her. These men, he assured her, had so much influence with their fellow-Jews that they could injure those whom they hated and help those to whom they were friendly; for they had the complete confidence of the masses when they spoke harshly of any person, even when they did so out of envy; and he himself, he added, had come into conflict with the nation because these men had been badly treated by him. (*AJ* 13.401f.)

She was even to entrust his corpse to their discretion and to promise them that "nothing would be done in the kingdom contrary to their will" (403). The queen accepted this counsel, handing his body and the kingdom over to them. "She made them favorably inclined toward herself, and they became friends" (405). Everywhere they sang hymns of praise for the dead king and lamented "that they had lost a righteous king," and in this way they brought about a splendid funeral with the people (405f.).

This text sketches the Pharisees much more negatively than the parallel passage *BJ* 1.112: They are dangerous and provoke unrest; they have great influence among the people—hypocrites without opinions of their own when they are able to achieve power. They misuse this power for the persecution of their opponents: "The whole country was quiet, with the exception of the Pharisees"

(*AJ* 13.410). Those who were persecuted by them could petition the queen, "if it seemed right to her to show preference to the Pharisees" (415), but only for sanctuary in the citadels.[7] Therefore, Aristobolus wanted to seize power during an illness of his mother, because he was afraid that after her death "the whole family would fall under the Pharisee's domination" (423). The critical posture of this whole text toward the Pharisees, is sharper, in contrast to the parallel in *BJ*. Is Nicolaus of Damascus (whose text Josephus reproduces here completely), behind this as well?

At the beginning of Herod's rule, Josephus explains that the king wanted to honor the Pharisee Pollio and his student Samias, because they had advised the citizens during the siege of Jerusalem to shelter Herod. Pollio also testified at Herod's trial before Hyrcanus II that Herod would proceed against them all if Herod were saved. Now God had fulfilled his word (15.3-4). Years later, Pollio, together with his pupils, refused to swear allegiance to Herod— apparently for religious reasons—but Herod permitted this to go unpunished (15.370). To the historian, this seems less a description of the Pharisees than a positive picture of a grateful Herod.

Very different are the angry Pharisees, who were introduced in conjunction with the reproach made against Pheroras's wife (see *BJ* 1.572) as if they had never been discussed before. Apparently, Josephus copied from Nicolaus here also.

> . . . whole Jewish people affirmed by an oath that it would be loyal to Caesar and to the king's government, these men, over six thousand in number, refused to take this oath, and when the king punished them with a fine, Pheroras' wife paid the fine for them. (*AJ* 17.41f.)

---

7. J. Neusner, "Josephus' Pharisees," 288, contrasts *AJ* with *BJ:* "The mass slaughter of War in which the Pharisees killed anyone they wanted, is shaded into a mild persecution of the Pharisees' opposition." Actually, these two pictures are not substantively different in this point. Where *BJ* 1.113 has "They kill (*aneroun*) whomever they want," *AJ* 13.410f. states "They tried to persuade them that they would kill those who had sided with Alexander . . . then they themselves killed one of them, Diogenes, and after him the remainder, one after another."

As a reward for this, they predicted that the throne of Herod would fall to her and her descendents. When Herod heard this, he executed the guiltiest of the Pharisees and the eunuch Bagoas, to whom they had promised a position of honor and descendants(!), as well as to a certain Karos and everyone from the royal household "who agreed with what the Pharisee said" (17.44). The singular probably means, as in 18.17, the group as a whole.

The Pharisees were portrayed in an extremely unfavorable light here.[8] They had much influence over prominent women and misused it as they had previously done with the naive Salome Alexandra. A few of them exploited the gentleness of the king—who was satisfied with a monetary penalty for their refusal to swear, a monetary penalty that Pheroras's wife paid for them—by making subversive speeches at the royal court, but even then only the guiltiest were executed.

The Pharisees were no longer mentioned during the time of Herod. At the time of direct Roman rule (6 C.E.) and concurrent property assessment, the high priest advised the people to flee. Judas of Gamala assured himself of the assistance of the Pharisee Zaddok and agitated the people to resist the Roman authorities (*AJ* 18.3f.). According to Josephus (18.10) their influence led ultimately to the destruction of Jerusalem and the Temple. He added a description of the three religious parties in exactly the same place as he had already done in *BJ* 2.118ff. There, however, he expressly emphasized that the new group of Judas the Galilean had nothing to do with the other three. Only here do we learn of the participation of a Pharisee in the revolt. Did Josephus intentionally omit the Pharisees not only from the uprising itself but also from the events preceding it?

In *AJ* 18.11 he listed the three philosophies that "the Jews had, according to patriarchal traditions, from ancient times" in an unusual sequence—Essenes, Sadducees, and Pharisees. He then proceeded to describe the Pharisees first:

---

8. Usually scholars refer back to Nicolaus of Damascus; thus D. R. Schwarz, *Josephus and Nicolaus,* 159f.); on the other hand, A. J. Saldarini, *Pharisees,* 99, n. 52: "Josephus is completely consistent in all his works in condemning troublemakers."

The Pharisees simplify their standard of living, making no conces-
sion to luxury. They follow the guidance of that which their doctrine
has selected and transmitted as good, attaching the chief importance
to the observance of those commandments which it has seen fit to
dictate to them. They show respect and deference to their elders, nor
do they rashly presume to contradict their proposals. (*AJ* 18.12)

As in *BJ* there follow references to Pharisaic ideas regarding the
relationship of free will, fate, and life after death.

Because of these views they are, as a matter of fact, extremely
influential among the townsfolk; and all prayers and sacred rites of
divine worship are performed according to their exposition. This is
the great tribute that the inhabitants of the cities, by practising the
highest ideals both in their way of living and in their discourse, have
paid to the excellence of the Pharisees.

The Sadducees hold that the soul perishes along with the body.
They own no observance of any sort apart from the laws; in fact,
they reckon it a virtue to dispute with the teachers of the path of
wisdom that they pursue. There are but few men to whom this doctrine has been made known, but these are men of the highest standing. They accomplish practically nothing, however. For whenever
they assume some office, though they submit unwillingly and per-
force, yet submit they do to the formulas of the Pharisees, since
otherwise the masses would not tolerate them. (*AJ* 18.15-17)

The Sadducees appear here also only as a contrast to the Pharisees. The completely positive characterization of the Pharisees is
their most comprehensive portrait in Josephus. It is even more thorough than that in *BJ* 2. The two temporally nonspecific texts, which
are only secondarily included with the events in the year 6 C.E., do
not quite coincide with the texts that record the Pharisees and Sadducees in political activity. Did Josephus incorporate a pro-Pharisee
propaganda text while he had previously relied especially on Nicolaus? Josephus does not seem particularly interested in reconciling
his sources. The text just cited, which is certainly intended to describe the Pharisees' influence on the masses in a positive way,
became a criticism when Josephus wrote in the passage just preceding that the movement cofounded by the Pharisee Zaddok and the

Galilean Judas had an unhealthy influence on the people. Actually, Josephus also said about Zaddok's "fourth philosophical school" that

> This school agrees in all other respects with the opinions of the Pharisees, except that they have a passion for liberty that is almost unconquerable, since they are convinced that God alone is their leader and master. (*AJ* 18.23)

The spiritual proximity admitted here between the Pharisees and the zealots also explains why some of the leading Pharisees joined the revolt against Rome. In *BJ* Josephus reported nothing about it, and he does not treat these years in *AJ*, but in the supplement—in his biography—he lists Pharisees by name. In *AJ* the Pharisees themselves disappeared from the story at the beginning of Roman rule. Josephus named only one Sadducee, in the year 62 C.E., Ananus, the son of Ananus, became the high priest. *BJ* 4.319-21 praises him in highest possible terms without mentioning any connection with the Sadducees. Here Josephus is rather critical.[9]

> The younger Ananus, who, as we have said, had been appointed to the high priesthood, was rash in his temper and unusually daring. He followed the school of the Sadducees, who are indeed more heartless than any of the other Jews, as I have already explained, when they sit in judgement. (*AJ* 20.199)

Ananus used the absence of the Roman governor to call the Sanhedrin into session and condemn James, the brother of Jesus. The text apparently refers to the scene under John Hyrcanus

---

9. S. J. D. Cohen, *Josephus,* 150f.: "High priests are treated much better by *BJ* than *AJ,* partly because *AJ* has its own political apologetic . . . , and partly because *AJ* was written by an adherent of the Phariasic view." G. Baumbach, *Das Sadduzäerverständnis,* 24, suggests that here "the anti-Sadducee orientation of *AJ* is clearly perceptible." On the other hand, A. J. Saldarini, *Pharisees,* 105: "Josephus is neither for nor against the Sadducees. . . . He supports order and praises anyone who resists the revolutionaries." But does this explain the shift in accent in *BJ?*

(*AJ* 13.293-96) where the moderation of the Pharisees in judgment was being discussed and contrasted with the attitude of the Sadducees. Along with Jonathan, who is mentioned there, is the younger Ananus, who is the only member of the Sadducees mentioned by Josephus by name.[10] The formulation used here does not mean "membership" in a Sadducee "party."

We find additional references to Pharisees in Josephus's autobiography. He writes that, after his return from Rome, he himself had been so thoroughly warned about an uprising that finally, regarding himself as a follower of Rome and his life as no longer safe, he, out of fear, sought protection in the inner court of the Temple. After the execution of the radical Menachem along with his most prominent followers, he came out again and met "with the high priests and the leaders of the Pharisees." Since they could not restrain the rebels, they decided to join them officially and try to restrain them until Cestius could restore order (*Vita* 20-23).

It seems that the leaders of the Jews joined the revolt only because of the circumstances. Josephus does not even say here that he belonged to the Pharisees. On the contrary, the Pharisees had proved to be his fundamental opponents. John of Gisala asked his old friend Simeon ben Gamaliel that Josephus be recalled from his command in Galilee.

> This Simon was a native of Jerusalem, of a very illustrious family, and of the sect of the Pharisees, who have the reputation of being unrivalled experts in their country's laws. A man highly gifted with intelligence and judgement, he could by sheer genius retrieve an unfortunate situation in affairs of state. (*Vita* 191f.)

Simeon actually tried to suggest the recall of Josephus to the high priests, Ananus and Jesus, son of Gamala, as well as a few of their party. Ananus hesitated at first, but he was bribed by John and he gave way to Simeon. They sent a delegation to Galilee,

10. J. Efron, *Studies,* 334-38 thinks that this section of the action of the Sadducee Ananus against James is a Christian interpolation. This cannot be proved. If Efron is correct, Jonathan would be the only Sadducee mentioned by name in Josephus.

a deputation comprising persons of different classes of society but of equal standing in education. Two of them, Jonathan and Ananias, were from the lower ranks and adherents of the Pharisees; the third, Jozar, also a Pharisee, came of a priestly family; the youngest, Simon, was descended from high priests. (*Vita* 196f.)

Thus the Pharisee Simeon ben Gamaliel, who was described in a very positive way, was one of the leaders of the insurrection in Jerusalem and was a friend of the radical John of Gisala. Three of the four members of the delegation sent at his instigation were Pharisees, and one of these was a priest (*BJ* 2.628 in part mentions other names and, above all, does not mention that there were three Pharisees among the four men). This shows quite clearly that the Pharisees had a leading role, at least in this phase of the revolt. This suggests that Josephus would not compromise the Pharisees or the high priests in front of the Romans in his description of the Jewish war. He even tried to make clear that it was not the leaders of the people but only a few irresponsible elements who drew the Palestinian Jews into the revolt against Rome. By this time, driven into a corner by his opponents, he lay aside his elegant reserve and named the Pharisee co-conspirators. Thus Josephus was apparently not a reliable comrade in arms, even though, as we mentioned at the beginning of this chapter, he had years before joined with the Pharisees in political affairs.

1.4 Summary

Compared with the description in *BJ*, Josephus offers a few bits of new information in *AJ* and its appendix, the *Vita*. Compared to the Pharisees, the Sadducees remain in the background, but they are more systematically presented to contrast to the Pharisees, and they appear as the Pharisees' opponents.[11] In the episode under John

---

11. The statement in J. Le Moyne, *Le Sadducéens,* 46, is questionable that the infrequent appearance of the Sadducees in Josephus "doit avoir, en partie, pour cause sa méfiance, voire son hostilité envers les Sadducéens." The explanation of A. J. Saldarini, *Pharisees,* 106, "because they have an impact on national leadership less often than the Pharisees," is also not satisfying.

Hyrcanus and in the form of the high priest Ananus the Younger (the execution of James), they maintain a kind of historic profile and thereby are described more negatively than in *BJ*.

Josephus took the history of the Pharisees farther back, describing them as ancient. He emphasized their adherence to tradition not chronicled in the Torah and their gentleness in the courts. He praised their influence over the masses, especially in the cities, and above all, over women. Even the Sadducees had to follow them when questions of cultic activity and prayer arose.[12] Their resistance to an oath of allegiance to Herod sounds like an uncompromising position regarding the relationship of religion and politics. The assertion that only their unbridled love of freedom distinguishes them from the so-called fourth philosphy also fits with this.

M. Smith understood the shift in accent from *BJ* to *AJ* regarding the Pharisees, especially the emphasis on their influence over the masses as a plea to the Roman authorities. On the question of which Jewish group they ought to support to keep the peace in Palestine, he writes, "Josephus is volunteering an answer: The Pharisees, he says, again and again, have by far the greatest influence with the people. Any government which secures their support is accepted; any government which alienates them has trouble."[13] Twenty years after the revolt, the Pharisees in Rome had a leading role, and Josephus supported them with his characterization in *AJ*.

This interpretation is not justified by the texts. Certainly, Josephus first emphasized the influence of the Pharisees on the masses in *AJ*. Nevertheless, he also showed what negative use they made of it. Even under Salome Alexandra, who granted them all powers, they are the only trouble spot. They also proved themselves to be a subversive element for Herod, who was close friends with a leading Pharisee. They were spiritual kin to the zealots. The temperate

---

12. J. Neusner, "Josephus' Pharisees," 282f., regards this as untenable, seeing in it the perspective of the decade of the destruction of Jerusalem when the Pharisees no longer had any power. This is neither impossible nor compelling.

13. M. Smith, *Palestinian Judaism,* 76. On Smith's thesis, see D. Goodblatt, *The Place of the Pharisees.*

branch of the Pharisees that tried to hold back the rebels in the year 66 C.E. did not have enough influence among the people in this decisive situation to be successful.[14] In the *Vita* Josephus showed even more clearly—including names—the entanglement of a succession of Pharisees in the rebellion.[15] It is here that Simeon ben Gamaliel, the father of Gamaliel of Jamnia, is exposed. Is this supposed to win friends in Rome for the Pharisees? Certainly, even if Josephus had wanted to, he could not simply have withdrawn his negative statements about the Pharisees at a later date in *AJ*. He even added another series of negative characteristics in *AJ*. Propaganda for the benefit of the Pharisees, which is how J. Neusner (in conjunction with M. Smith) characterizes the description in *AJ*, would have to look quite different.[16]

14. D. R. Schwartz, *Josephus and Nicolaus,* 164ff., correctly emphasizes that the apologetic in the portrayal of the Pharisees in *BJ* is much clearer than in *AJ*, where Josephus is no longer so careful and no longer suppresses sources that contradict his own perceptions. The passages in *AJ* on the political influence of the Pharisees would hardly play well among the Romans.

15. If we, as does Neusner, accept H. St. J. Thackery's dating of the *Vita* (Loeb Classical Library, *Josephus* 1 [Cambridge, 1926], XIIf.), that is, after 100 C.E.—we should not without further ado combine their comments with the statements in *AJ*. Nevertheless, this late dating is not certain, and *AJ* is not generally friendly toward the Pharisees. For an earlier dating of the *Vita* see, for example, A. J. Saldarini, *Pharisees,* 82, who states that *AJ* and the *Vita* were produced together in 93–94 C.E., after the death of Agrippa.

16. J. Neusner, "Josephus' Pharisees," 290. L. H. Feldman, in the introduction to the volume in which Neusner's essay appears, calls attention to the lack of uniformity in Josephus's description and the negative features also in *AJ*. The description of the Pharisees at the time of Salome Alexandra "as evil geniuses who are ruthless in cutting down their opponents, could hardly strike the reader as enhancing their cause" (50). S. N. Mason, *Was Josephus a Pharisee?* 45, also clearly reverts to the thesis of a pro-Pharisee apologetic in *AJ* and the *Vita:* "Such an apologetic does not exist in these works." S. D. Cohen, *Josephus,* 151, n. 171, sees correctly that there are also passages in *AJ* "which are quite nasty to the Pharisees." This makes Cohen's position that Josephus was actually associated with the Pharisaic movement in the 90s quite doubtful.

2. THE NEW TESTAMENT

A cursory examination of the writings of the New Testament—in chronological order—should detail the trends and possible shifts in the portrait of the Pharisees. Only the earliest text, which is Paul's labeling of himself as a Pharisee in Phil. 3:5, is more useful in combination with the statements in Acts. Even more than in Josephus, the Pharisees are the dominant group in the New Testament, while the Sadducees recede into the background. In spite of Acts 5:17, where the Sadducees stand with the high priests, we are not justified in automatically filling out the portrait of the Sadducees with statements by the high priests,[17] if the texts do not expressly designate them as Sadducees.

2.1 The Gospel according to Mark

Mark mentioned the Sadducees only one time, and that is in the question regarding the resurrection (Mark 12:18-27). Their denial of the resurrection shows that they "know neither the scriptures nor the power of God" (12:24), and for that reason they are very confused.[18] The polemic statement that the Sadducees do not know the Bible is repeated in rabbinic literature and may refer to differing methods of biblical interpretation. Jesus' only contact with the Sadducees recorded in the Bible happened in Jerusalem, and the text gives no possibility of a justification for their standpoint.

The Pharisees, mentioned twelve times in Mark, usually appear in Galilee. In 2:16 the "scribes of the Pharisees" criticize Jesus for eating with tax collectors and sinners. In 2:18 some of the nonfasting disciples of Jesus are contrasted with those of John and the Pharisees (or the disciples of the Pharisees), who fasted.[19] In 2:23ff. again the Pharisees take offense that Jesus' disciples are picking stalks of grain on the Sabbath. The scene that follows directly (3:1-6), in which Jesus heals a man with a withered hand in the

---

17. Thus, for example, G. Baumbach, *Jesus,* 62.
18. For this, see O. Schwankl, *Die Sadduzäerfrage.*
19. D. Lührmann, *The Pharisees,* 178. The comparison with John's disciples is probably only secondarily transferred to the Pharisees.

synagogue on the Sabbath, includes the closing sentence, "The Pharisees went out and immediately conspired with the Herodians against him, how to destroy him." With that Mark labels the Pharisees as Jesus' mortal enemies at the very beginning of his public ministry, for they were unable to accept his understanding of the Law.

Mark 7:1-13 indicts the Pharisees for falsifying the word of God with their notions of the Law, and this passage suggests that their religious efforts were not altogether honorable. "The Pharisees and some of the scribes who had come from Jerusalem" came to Jesus and complained that Jesus' disciples did not wash their hands before eating, as "the Pharisees and all the Jews" (7:3), and thereby went against the tradition of the elders. Jesus dismissed them as hypocrites to whom Isa. 29:3 applies; that is, they replaced God's law with their own traditions, in many cases rendering the explicit words of the Torah impotent by their exposition.

After the miracle of the loaves the Pharisees began another argument with Jesus, demanding from him a sign, but he ignored them (8:11-13) and warned his disciples about "the yeast of the Pharisees and the yeast of Herod" (8:15). Afterward, Jesus left Galilee and came to Judea, in the region across the Jordan, where the Pharisees met him again to set a trap for him by asking him whether divorce is permissible. Jesus told them that contrary to the created order, Moses had permitted it, but only because of their hardheartedness (10:1-9). One final time, "some Pharisees and some Herodians" (12:13) tried to lure him into a trap with the question whether it is permitted to pay tax to Caesar. But Jesus, recognizing "their hypocrisy . . . said to them, 'Why are you putting me to the test?'"

Since Josephus frequently portrayed the Pharisees as precise interpreters of the law, their connection with (the) scribes is to be expected. This group appears more frequently, and they are apparently more important than the Pharisees in Mark. The Pharisees assume a dominant role only in the later Gospels. The association with the disciples of John (probably a later redaction) is more remarkable, and even more so is that with Herod (Antipas) and the Herodians—apparently his partisans. Did Mark reproduce the historical relationship here, or was it his intention to suggest that for the Pharisees everyone who opposed Jesus was an ally?

We will discuss the points of controversy between Jesus and the Pharisees—Sabbath rest, purity, table fellowship with tax collectors and sinners, divorce—in the next section. Josephus's statements do not prepare us for these directly, but rather in general, through the common emphasis on the Pharisaic tradition. Since the legal questions mentioned here also play a part in the early rabbinic tradition, Mark is usually seen as reliable evidence for the Pharisees' points of concern. Nevertheless, Mark is apparently not much concerned with realism and objectivity: the Pharisees (like the Sadducees) served simply as a schematically drawn group to contrast negatively with Jesus and his disciples. Both groups are always described in negative terms in Mark. The Sadducees do not understand the Bible, and the Pharisees are always trying to trap Jesus. In reality, their tradition emphasizes God's word in many points; their religious zeal is hypocrisy. It is all the more remarkable, then, that the Pharisees, who from the very beginning were described as Jesus' mortal enemies, do not appear in the Passion narrative.

2.2 The Q Material

Sadducees do not appear in Q, the source common to Matthew and Luke, and only two passages about the Pharisees can be traced with confidence to Q.[20] Both continue the same polemic known from Mark. In one (Matt. 23:23; Luke 11:42), Jesus scolds them about their forgetfulness of the essence of the Torah in their tithing; in the other (Matt. 23:25; Luke 11:39), he reproaches them for the superficiality of their prescriptions for purity. The second point was already central in Mark, where it was first advanced in the discussion of table fellowship. Matt. 23:2, 6 (see Luke 11:43) might also be connected with this. Here the scribes and Pharisees occupy the chair of Moses; they love the place of honor at table and in the synagogue and want to be greeted there (but compare Mark 12:38f.!). This corresponds in substance with Josephus's recognition of their

---

20. S. H. Brooks, *Matthew's Community* (Sheffield, 1987), 27, correctly emphasizes how rarely Matthew and Luke coincide on statements about the Pharisees. This makes it probable "that Q did not contain the same emphasis on the opposition of the Pharisees developed independently by both Matthew and Luke."

authority in interpretation and their influence on the cult. We probably ought to think of their statements about banquets as an effort to control in questions regarding purity and the practice of tithing; otherwise it would be a mere reproach for excessive efforts for honor and recognition. The accusation of hypocrisy in Matt. 23:23, 25 is missing in the Lukan parallel and thus may be attributed to Matthew.

2.3 Matthew

The Pharisees appear in Matthew more frequently than in the other writings of the New Testament (thirty times), but the Sadducees are also found more frequently because Matthew combines them into a single group. Matt. 3:7-10 already says that "many Pharisees and Sadducees" came to John for baptism; he called them a "brood of vipers," and they had to listen to his sermon of threats. Since Luke 3:7-9 also includes this sermon—but there it is directed toward the crowds—Matthew himself apparently added the combined group to Q.[21] In the demand for a sign, the Matt. 16:1 parallel to Mark 8:11 adds the Sadducees to the Pharisees (in Matt. 12:38 some scribes and Pharisees demand a sign). Together they must listen, because they do not know how to interpret the signs of the times. Finally, where Mark 8:15 warns of the yeast of the Pharisees and of Herod, Matt. 16:11f. (without parallel) explains the "yeast of the Pharisees and Sadducees" as "the teaching of the Pharisees and Sadducees." The article, always used of the two groups in common, underscores the idea that they belong together. Thus Matthew's clear understanding of the difference between the teachings of the groups seems inconsequential to him.[22]

---

21. G. Baumbach, *Jesus*, 49, speaks of a "questionable redactional coordination"; A. J. Saldarini, *Pharisee*, 157: "a historically opposed and thus improbable pair according to some scholars." He does say that the Pharisees and Sadducees had common interests, and their conflicts may have been exaggerated (167, 173).

22. I do not believe that we can reduce the statements on the question of the Messiah's task—out of context—to a single position for both Pharisees and Sadducees, as H. W. Hoehner, *Herod Antipas*, 213, does: "a purely external-nationalistic political kingdom." What evidence is there, outside of New Testament polemic, for this position of the two groups?

On the other hand, Matthew repeatedly says that the Pharisees alone were responsible. Where Mark 3:6 has the Pharisees together with the Herodians plotting the assassination of Jesus, Matt. 12:14 has the Pharisees acting by themselves. Indeed, in the tax question, Matt. 22:15f. and Mark 12:13 list the Pharisees and the Herodians together, but the Pharisees predominate because they were the initiators. In comparison with Mark, in Matthew the Herodians are less important in the role of allies of the Pharisees. Whether this can be substantiated by altered historical conditions is debatable in view of the unhistorical combination of Pharisees and Sadducees. It is probably more important to Matthew to emphasize the role of the Pharisees. We see this again in Matt. 9:11; unlike Mark 2:16, "the scribes of the Pharisees" (Luke 5:30, "the Pharisees and their scribes), it is simply "the Pharisees" who reproach Jesus for his eating with tax collectors and sinners. Only in Matt. 9:11 does Jesus answer them with Hos. 6:6, "I desire steadfast love and not sacrifice," thereby attributing to them the opposite position. The statement following Jesus' remark that he did not come to give prominence to the law or the prophets is without parallel: "Unless your righteousness exceeds that of the scribes and Pharisees, you will never enter the kingdom of heaven" (5:20). In this statement the Pharisees are granted at least some degree of righteousness; it simply is not enough. Since Matthew so readily connects scribes and Pharisees, some manuscripts likewise add the Pharisees secondarily in 7:29: "He taught them as one having authority, not as their scribes."

Only Matthew puts the accusation that Jesus drove out demons with the help of demons in the mouth of the Pharisees (Matt. 9:34; 12:24; Mark 3:22, "the scribes who came down from Jerusalem"; Luke 11:15, "some" of the crowd; compare John 7:20; 8:48, 52; 10:20). In Matthew's version of the debate about the greatest commandment, we see especially clearly how omnipresent the Pharisees are in his Gospel. Here Matthew, like Mark, recounts this story following the defeat of the Sadducees in the discussion of the resurrection. Where Mark 12:28 has "one of the scribes" inquiring of Jesus in all honesty and receiving approval from him that he was not far from the kingdom of God, in Matthew the entire scene changes into one of hostility: "When the Pharisees heard that he had silenced the Sadducees, they gathered together, and one of them, a lawyer, asked him a question to test him" (22:34f.):[23] Which is the greatest commandment? Thus the Pharisees had to be taught about the essential content of the law, as though they had no knowledge of it.

Since the Pharisees were already with Jesus, he asked them in 22:41f. what they think about the Messiah (in Mark 12:35 and Luke 20:41 the question is associated with the the scribes). Thus it is also the Pharisees who were unable to answer his use of Ps. 110:1: "No one was able to give him an answer, nor from that day did anyone dare to ask him any more questions" (22:46). Mark concludes the section on the greatest commandment with a corresponding statement. Luke places it at the end of a discussion with the Sadducees. When Matthew ends the discussion of the Pharisees with this, he emphasizes that the Pharisees were rendered speechless: at least theologically speaking, their coalition was finished.

In Matt. 23:1-26 Jesus settled his accounts with the scribes and the Pharisees (the substantive parallels in Mark 12:37-40 and Luke 20:45-47 are directed only at the scribes). The beginning of chapter 23 in the context of the preceding chapter is remarkable, "The scribes and the Pharisees sit on Moses' seat" (23:2f.). Thus their teaching is authentic and binding; it is only what they do that provokes criticism. They do not bear the real burden of the law: they are concerned only with external appearance. They are ambitious, blind leaders, who block the way to the kingdom of heaven for others. They are disobedient to the will of God. The accusation of hypocrisy occurs regularly among the insults. This is a favorite motif in Matthew (the phrase appears ten times in Matthew and secondarily in Matt. 23:14, twice in Mark, and four times in Luke).[24] Half of the cases are directed toward (the scribes and) the Pharisees. Mark is already acquainted with the accusation, having used it in

---

23. In Luke 10:25 a certain teacher of the law asks Jesus this question as a test, but in another context. Since Matthew, like Luke, uses the term *nomikos* only here, the negative interpretation of the section through *(ek)peirazōn* may go back to a common tradition.

24. See U. Wilckens, S.V. *"hypokrinomai," TWNT* 8:566.

7:6 and 12:15 against the Pharisees. Luke points to the yeast of the Pharisees as hypocrisy. The motif is apparently older: there is a parallel in the report of Josephus regarding the behavior of the Pharisees at the beginning of the reign of Salome Alexandra (see also *Sota* 22b), and at least in individual cases, it could be behind the expression usually directed at the Pharisees in the Qumran texts—*dorshe halaqot.* Thus the term may be more widely used.

Unlike Mark, in Matthew the Pharisees remain in the foreground even during Jesus' stay in Jerusalem. "The high priests and the Pharisees" relate Jesus' parables to themselves and decide to have him arrested, but they are afraid of the people (21:45f.; Mark 12:12 says simply "they," which in conjunction with 11:27 means "the high priests, the scribes, and the elders"; Luke 20:19, "the scribes and the Pharisees"). Matthew does not mention them in Jesus' trial. Nevertheless, Matt. 27:62—without parallel—includes the remark that after the death of Jesus, the leading priests and the Pharisees went to Pilate to request a guard for Jesus' tomb, so that no mischief can occur.

In general, the Pharisees are the regular, ever-present, principal enemies of Jesus. They are largely indistinguishable from the Sadducees. But they are combined even more frequently (nine times) with the scribes,[25] for which reason they are less important as an independent force than in Mark, since Matthew accepts the exist-

---

25. R. Hummel, *Die Auseinandersetzung,* 14f., regards this combination of "scribes and Pharisees" as not wholly unjustified, insofar as the majority of the scribes were among the Pharisees. Above all, Matthew was acquainted only with Pharisaic scribes. Hummel's (along with Jeremias's) juxtaposition of the ordained scribes (already before 70 C.E.!) against the ordinary members of the Pharisaic *haburah,* suggesting that "there is no noticeable distinction between leaders and followers in Matthew" (15), is indeed questionable. From Josephus onward we must generally regard the Pharisees as trained experts in the Law and tradition, which can be seen also in their small numbers relative to their influence. For an identification of the scribes and the Pharisees, see E. Rivkin, *A Hidden Revolution,* 105ff. (likewise *HUCA* 49 [1978]: 135–42); for a differentiation see D. R. Schwartz, *Scribes:* at least sometimes the *grammateus* (as in LXX) is simply a lower-ranking official; likewise A. J. Saldarini, *Pharisees,* 264ff. See also R. Hayward, "Some Notes in the Targum to the Prophets," *JJS* 36 (1985): 210-21.

ence of Christian scribes. The sketchy use of the Pharisees in this portrait scarcely permits itself to be evaluated for a historical reconstruction extending beyond the facts known from Mark and Q. It is rather of interest for a picture of the enemy of the Christian community that Matthew represents. For this purpose the Pharisees especially are the biblically trained representatives of Judaism, from whom the Sadducees are distinguished only by clichés.[26]

2.4 Luke

Like Mark, Luke mentions the Sadducees in his Gospel only in the discussion of the resurrection. In contrast, he introduces the Pharisees twenty-seven times—many of them without parallel in Matthew or Mark. He also gives us a different picture of them. This is already shown in that he does not simply refer summarily to "the Pharisees," but also "some of the Pharisees" (for example, 6:2 compared with Mark 2:24 and Matt. 12:2: "the Pharisees" in the question of Sabbath gleaning), or he distinguishes individual Pharisees.

Occasionally, Luke modifies statements from the other two parallel traditions. Whereas in Mark 3:6 the Pharisees consult with the Herodians (in Matt. 12:14 it is the Pharisees alone), on how they might do away (*apolesōsin*) with Jesus, Luke 6:7, 11 mentions "the scribes and the Pharisees" who, "filled with fury" (6:11), took counsel as to what they might be able to do (*poiēsaien*) against Jesus. In Luke 11:16 it was not the Pharisees who demanded of Jesus a sign, as in Mark 8:11 and Matt. 16:1 (together with the Sadducees), but simply "others."

The table fellowship that Jesus enjoyed with Pharisees, repeatedly mentioned by Luke alone, is most interesting. Thus "one of the Pharisees" invited Jesus to a meal (7:36; his name, Simon, is not

---

26. R. Hummel, *Die Auseinandersetzung,* 14. The dominance of the Pharisees after the destruction of the Temple mirrors Matthew's use of the Pharisees as the actual opponents of Jesus. Matthew included this in the life of Jesus in respect of the tradition.

mentioned until verse 40; Mark 14:3 and Matt. 26:26 call the host Simon the leper).[27] The Pharisee, observing how Jesus sat at the feet of the sinful woman, reflected, "If this man were a prophet . . ." (7:39). Jesus praised the woman's love to Simon. Because of that love, her many sins were forgiven.

Whereas in Mark 7:1 and Matt. 15:1 the scribes and Pharisees observe from the outside that a few of Jesus' disciples had not washed their hands before eating and then the Pharisees complain about it, Luke 11:37f. transfers the scene into the context of an invitation and thereby reduces the level of hostility. A Pharisee invites Jesus, who was already on the way to Jerusalem, to dinner. The Pharisee is amazed that he did not wash his hands before eating. Jesus answers with an attack on the Pharisees, who only clean themselves externally. They are quite exact about the tithe, but not about essential things; and they want to have the prominent seats in the synagogue, and so on (11:39, 42, 43). The parallels in Matt. 23:25, 23, 6 show that Luke arranged material here from Q to meet his own needs. Against the objection of a teacher of the law (*nomikos*), Jesus upbraids the lawyers (11:45-52). The scene ends so that "the scribes and the Pharisees began to be very hostile toward him and to cross-examine him about many things" (11:53). Immediately thereafter, Jesus warns about the "yeast of the Pharisees, that is, their hypocrisy" (12:1). Nevertheless, it is still only "some Pharisees" who come to Jesus and warn him, "Get away from here, for Herod wants to kill you" (13:31, completely without parallel; there is no trace of a negative connotation).[28] Jesus is also the guest of a

---

27. J. A. Ziesler, *Luke*, 150, suggests that Luke "deliberately modifies his inherited anti-Pharisaic tradition by creating these host-guest contexts." He certainly did not minimize the theological distance between Jesus and the Pharisees in his Gospel, but he might ascribe to them a less hostile attitude toward Jesus. According to Ziesler this indicates that the Pharisees were not so hostile toward the church in Luke's time: "His tendency may be his creation, but it is unlikely to be ex nihilo" (156).

28. Compare J. A. Ziesler, *Luke*, 149f. U. Luz, *Jesus*, 240, sees in this text within the Gospel a "single ancient tradition that localizes the Pharisees in Galilee."

Pharisee in 14:1. "On one occasion when Jesus was going to the house of a Pharisee to eat a meal on the sabbath, they were watching him closely," whether he would heal on the Sabbath. "And Jesus asked the lawyers (*nomikoi*) and Pharisees, 'Is it lawful to cure people on the sabbath, or not?'" (14:3).

Based on these invitations, one must conclude that Jesus' relations with the Pharisees could not have been as bad as they are portrayed in the other Gospels. Furthermore, the differences between Jesus and the Pharisees on questions of ritual purity must not have been so great, if we look at the scenes described by other writers in addition to Luke. In two of the three scenes ritual purity is not discussed at all.

In two of the invitation narratives teachers of the law are also present. Wherever they (or the scribes) are associated with the Pharisees, the disagreements are always over *halakah* or teaching. For Luke alone the Pharisees are critical questioners; nevertheless, they are not direct opponents of Jesus. Since the Pharisees appear primarily together with scribes (and other similar people), it is remarkable that Luke introduces independent Pharisees in negative scenes where the accusation is directed only at the scribes. Thus only Luke adds a Pharisee in the narrative of healing of the lame man. While Jesus was teaching, "Pharisees and teachers of the law were sitting near by (they had come from every village in Galilee and Judea and from Jerusalem)" (5:17); since Jesus offered forgiveness of sins to the lame man, "the scribes and the Pharisees began to question . . ." (5:21).

Together, the scribes and the Pharisees complained that Jesus ate with tax collectors and sinners (5:30, so also 15:2—here as an introduction to the parable of the lost sheep, which is also included in Matt. 18:12-14). They watch him to see whether he would heal on the Sabbath (6:7). Luke 7:30 is without parallel and even contradicts Matt. 3:7 when it states that—in contrast to the whole people and even the tax collectors—"by refusing to be baptized by him [John], the Pharisees and the lawyers [*nomikoi*] rejected God's purpose for themselves" (7:30) (see also above, Luke 11:53).

The statement in Luke 16:14 about "the Pharisees, who were lovers of money" (and for that reason they derided Jesus' statements about the kingdom) is without parallel in the Gospels.[29] Jesus answers the Pharisees, "You are those who justify yourselves in the sight of others; but God knows your hearts; for what is prized by human beings is an abomination in the sight of God" (16:15). Certainly, Luke's ideal of poverty plays a part here, but we are not justified in judging the Pharisees to be lovers of money because they did not accept that role. The question of when the kingdom of God would come (17:20) is without parallel in the Gospels, as is the parable of the Pharisee and the tax collector in the Temple, in which the Pharisee boasts that, unlike the tax collectors and sinners, he fasts twice each week and he tithes of all his possessions (18:10-12). The Pharisee is sketched here as a caricature, but the positive statements made about him may still be taken seriously.

A final mention of the Pharisees occurs at Jesus' entry into Jerusalem, where "some of the Pharisees in the crowd" demand that Jesus order his disciples to be quiet (19:39). When taxes are discussed (20:20), the Pharisees are no longer mentioned. They also play no part in the Passion narrative.[30]

In Acts Luke also speaks more frequently of the Pharisees—always positively—while the Sadducees are opponents of the Christian community. "The high priest took action; he and all who were with him (that is, the sect [*hairesis*] of the Sadducees)" (5:17) had the apostles arrested. In the meeting of the Sanhedrin with the *gerousia* (5:21), which was supposed to deal with the accusations

29. J. T. Sanders, *The Jews,* 93, regards this as slander, showing "that Luke has a profound dislike for the Pharisees and that he thinks of them as making light of Jesus, but the grounds for both escape us." Nevertheless, Sanders also emphasizes (84ff.) that Luke narrows the differences between the Pharisees and Jesus, even seeing differences among the Pharisees. Occasionally *AJ* 17.42, where Pheroras's wife pays the fine for the Pharisees, is taken as an additional reference to the Pharisee's love of money, but this text cannot be used in so clearly defined a manner.

30. D. P. Moessner, "The 'Leaven of the Pharisees,'" suggests that in the Passion narrative the scribes are to be understood clearly as those of the Pharisees (38), but they are not explicitly named, because Luke, who refers in Acts to Christian Pharisees, consciously wants to distinguish between the groups in the church (42f.).

against the apostles, "a Pharisee in the council named Gamaliel, a teacher of the law, respected by all the people" arose and advised the people to let the men have their way; if their plan was of purely human origin, it would fail, but if the plan were from God, they would be powerless against it (5:34, 38f.). The young Christian community could hardly have hoped for someone with better intentions.[31]

Before the Sanhedrin, Paul himself appeals to his Pharisee past:

> When Paul noticed that some were Sadducees and others were Pharisees, he called out in the council, "Brothers, I am a Pharisee, a son of Pharisees. I am on trial concerning the hope of the resurrection of the dead." When he said this, a dissension began between the Pharisees and the Sadducees, and the assembly was divided. (The Sadducees say that there is no resurrection, or angel, or spirit; but the Pharisees acknowledge all three.) Then a great clamor arose, and certain scribes of the Pharisees' group stood up and contended, "We find nothing wrong with this man. What if a spirit or an angel has spoken to him?" (Acts 23:6-9)

It is remarkable that Luke here speaks of Paul as a Pharisee in the present, "I *am* a Pharisee."[32] When called before Agrippa, Paul appeals to his Pharisaic *past*: ". . . if they are willing to testify, that I have belonged to the strictest sect of our religion and lived as a Pharisee" (26:5). We can also cite the statement in Phil. 3:5, according to which Paul was *kata nomon pharisaisos*.[33] If we can take historically this information from Acts, it means that the early community in Jerusalem could hope for prospects of goodwill from the

31. It is hard to say to what extent the description of Gamaliel is historically accurate, because Luke's concern to show a continuity between Pharisaic Judaism and the Christian community also plays a part.

32. J. A. Ziesler, *Luke*, 146f., correctly relates the statement especially to the testimony to the resurrection that for Luke is the center of the gospel: "As Luke conceives the gospel, the Sadducees are its enemies, and the Pharisees are its friends" (146); he does not maintain, however, that there is further theological unity.

33. Occasionally it is doubted how far Paul, as a diaspora Jew, could be considered an actual Pharisee. Discussions about it are naturally connected to the

leaders of the Pharisees. Against this background we may also understand the narratives in the Gospels of the close contacts between Jesus and the Pharisees in Galilee. Thus some Pharisees, according to Acts 15:5, were even members of the Christian community:

> But some believers who belonged to the seat [*hairesis*] of the Pharisees stood up [in the apostolic council in Jerusalem] and said, "It is necessary for them [the Gentile Christians] to be circumcised and ordered to keep the law of Moses."

This is the only place in Acts where the Pharisees cause problems, and these are Pharisees that had come over to Christianity! In the long run, the Pharisees had not been able to enforce their position at the apostolic council (in regard to the option of freedom from the law), even though they had been significant initially. If it were possible, using various arguments, to doubt that Paul had been a Pharisee at first, it would still be difficult to question the role of the Pharisees among the first Christians. What reason might Luke have had for such a position, if corresponding tendencies did not exist? This might shed some light on the anti-Pharisee polemic in the Gospel tradition, especially in Matthew and John. Is this not at least partially an intra-Christian polemic in the process of the community freeing itself from the roots of the law? It is not contradictory that we find the polemic especially sharp in the Gospels to which we credit a Jewish-Christian background. It was there that the problem of differentiation was greatest! This does not mean, however, that in Luke we ought to connect the argument between Jesus and the Pharisees first and foremost to Jewish Christians who still clung firmly to the Law.[34]

---

larger problems of the Pauline biography, which we are unable to discuss here. The opinion of H. Maccoby in *The Mythmaker: Paul and the Invention of Christianity* (New York, 1986) is misleading. According to Maccoby, in reality Paul was a member of the Sadducean Temple police, and as such he had been sent to Damascus. On this, see E. Rivkin, "Paul's Jewish Odyssey," *Judaism 38* (1989): 225–34. On Paul as a Pharisee, K. Berger, *Jesus,* 251–54, and A. J. Saldarini, *Pharisees,* 134–43 differ.

34. This is the rather one-sided tendency of J. T. Sanders: "Jesus' Pharisaic

2.5 John

Jesus' opponents in John are usually generically labeled "the Jews"; nevertheless, the Pharisees are also mentioned twenty times (including the not original scene with the adulteress whom "scribes and Pharisees" bring to Jesus in 8:3). They play a decisive role, while the Sadducees do not appear.[35] In general, John views the Pharisees as the leaders of the Jewish people. The emissaries who were sent to John the Baptist, according to John 1:19, consisted of priests and Levites. Still, 1:24 adds the comment, "Now they had been sent from the Pharisees,"[36] who asked John why he baptized and whether he was the Messiah or just a prophet. John 3:1 describes Nicodemus in a completely positive manner: "Now there was a Pharisee named Nicodemus, a leader of the Jews." His contact with Jesus at night probably shows that he did not want to compromise his position.

In 4:1 the Pharisees could be regarded as a threat: "Now when Jesus learned that the Pharisees had heard, 'Jesus is making more disciples than John' . . . he left Judea and started back to Galilee" (4:1-3). Does this passage mean that Galilee was not within the Pharisees' sphere of influence? Such a view would depart from that of the other three Gospels; indeed, in John the Pharisees do not appear outside of Judea.

---

opponents in the Gospels *stand for* traditionally Jewish Christians" (*The Jews*, 96); "The leaven of hypocrisy is the attempt of traditionally Jewish Christians to get Gentile Christians to follow the Torah" (111). See also R. A. Wild, *The Encounter*, 113ff.; J. T. Carroll, *Luke's Portrayal*, distinguishes more sharply between the conflict in the Gospels and the positive description in Acts. K. Berger, *Jesus*, 254ff., in my opinion uses too broad a concept of Pharisees and consequently is able to say more about the so-called diaspora Pharisees than the sources warrant.

35. The thesis of D. E. H. Whiteley, that the writer of John might have been a Sadducee who first adopted faith in Jesus and then in the resurrection, is pure speculation.

36. The text here is not completely clear, but the intent is that some Pharisees belonged to the delegation, not that they did the sending or that they sent their own delegation. See R. Schnackenburg, *Das Johannesevangelium* 1 (Freiburg, 1965), 280f.

During the Feast of Tabernacles in Jerusalem, when many people began to surmise that Jesus was the Messiah, the Pharisees heard about it. "The chief priests and Pharisees sent temple police to arrest him" (7:32). When they returned empty-handed to the "chief priests and Pharisees" (7:45), the latter accused them, "Surely you have not been deceived too, have you? Has any one of the authorities or of the Pharisees believed in him?" (7:47f.). Nevertheless, only the people who did not know the law had done so! Only then does Nicodemus introduce himself, seeking a fair judgment (7:50-52).

In 8:13 the Pharisees clash with Jesus in the Temple. They accuse him of testifying on his own behalf, which is not valid. On the way from the Temple, Jesus heals the man born blind, whom the people then bring to the Pharisees, because the healing took place on the Sabbath. The Pharisees do not recognize the miraculous sign, since Jesus did not observe the Sabbath (9:13-16). To the scornful question put by the man who was healed, "Do you also want to become his disciples?" the Pharisees reply, "We are disciples of Moses. We know that God has spoken to Moses, but as for this man, we do not know where he comes from" (9:27-29). In the meantime, a few Pharisees heard Jesus speak about the judgment through which the blind see and those who see become blind, and they asked Jesus, "'Surely we are not blind, are we?' Jesus said to them, 'If you were blind, you would not have sin. But now that you say, "We see," your sin remains'" (9:40f.).

After Jesus raised Lazarus, a few people told the Pharisees what Jesus had done. "The chief priests and the Pharisees called a meeting of the council" and decided to kill Jesus. "Now the chief priests and the Pharisees had given orders that anyone who knew where Jesus was should let them know, so that they might arrest him" (11:46f., 57). At Jesus' entry into Jerusalem, the Pharisees comment, "Look, the world has gone after him" (12:19). And in spite of the blindness of the people, evidenced in Isa. 53:1; 6:9f., "many, even of the authorities, believed in him. But because of the Pharisees they did not confess it, for fear that they would be put out of the synagogue; for they loved human glory more than the glory that comes from God" (John 12:42f.). The quotation from Isaiah plays a part in all the Gospels, but only in John is a connection made with the Pharisees. The statement about the Pharisees in 12:42 is made to refer to the Jews in general in 9:22, as if the two terms were interchangeable and the Pharisees were the representatives of Judaism.

John refers to the Pharisees one last time, in 18:3, at Jesus' arrest: "So Judas brought a detachment of soldiers together with police from the chief priests and the Pharisees, and they came there with lanterns and torches and weapons." In Mark 14:43 the people who arrested Jesus came "from the chief priests and the elders"; in Matt. 26:47, "from the chief priest and the elders of the people." Luke gives no further information, later mentioning—with the other Gospels—the servant of the high priest whom Peter wounded.

Thus far, it is clear that John represents the Pharisees as the driving force among the people, the men who mattered. For the most part, they are a group united with the the high priests, but usually the initiative comes from the Pharisees.[37] In this way, John exceeds the portrayal of the Pharisees in the Synoptics by a wide margin. He seems to know nothing about the Pharisees who had come to the faith (Acts), with the exception of Nicodemus, who made a public profession only very late. Indeed, he explicitly maintains the contrary. This is not the place to go into John's theology. Nevertheless, it is clear that John apparently schematized and limned the historical relationships at the time of Jesus intentionally, in order to project the situation of his community at the end of the century as a second level over the life of Jesus. It is enticing to try to find a concrete historical context, in which the Pharisees (or their later development in the decades after 70 C.E.) were the only Jewish opponents of the Johannine community.[38] We see frequently in John a reaction to rabbinic decisions in Yavneh (the so-called Council of Jamnia).[39] In so doing we cross the bounds of what is provable. It is

37. See J. Ashton, "The Identity and Function of the *Ioudaioi* in the Fourth Gospel," *NovT* 27 (1985): 40-75, especially 57ff.

38. U. Luz, *Jesus,* 240, correctly emphasizes that "the Pharisees became increasingly more significant in the strata that are redactional and late in traditional history."

39. Thus especially in J. L. Martyn, *History and Theology in the Fourth Gospel* (Nashville, 1968), 72ff.

probably better to be satisfied with the statement that John took over the cipher "the Pharisees" from the Jesus tradition to designate in general the Jewish authorities who set themselves against the mission efforts of the Christians by appeal to the Bible and their correct intepretation. For various reasons we suggest that the Johannine community was localized in the Galilean-Syrian border region. This could explain the statement of 4:1-3 that Jesus retreated from the Pharisees into Galilee.

2.6 Summary

Within the New Testament writings we can establish a clear development in the statements about the Pharisees, while the Sadducees never get beyond the cliché of denying the resurrection.[40] Already in Mark the Pharisees are the substantive opposition to Jesus, wanting to have him killed right from the beginning; by the Passion narrative, however, they no longer play a part. The points of conflict are the traditions of the fathers and the use of these traditions in resolving individual questions regarding the law. From a Christian point of view, the Pharisees were condemned as hypocrites. Their religiosity was seen as ignoring the essentials and emphasizing incidentals. Matthew continues this line; he gives positive emphasis, however, to their teaching authority, since some of Jesus' followers were Pharisees. Mark allows the Pharisees to appear more in the foreground, playing a role even in the beginning and the end of the Passion narrative, but not in the narrative itself. Compared to this, the Lukan description is surprising; in the banquet scenes, Luke emphasizes the closeness of the Pharisees to Jesus, and in Acts he clarifies the points of association between the Pharisees and the Christian community. By contrast, John is very different. He concentrates on the questions of the Sabbath and the Messiah, seeing the Pharisees as the representatives of the Jews. They are deluded and resist faith in Jesus, representing the hostile world for Christians. There is no room for nuance here.

---

40. This is perhaps partially determined by an "actualizing substitute system of the Synoptic tradition" that replaced Sadducees with Phariseees, K. Müller, *Jesus,* 24. Unfortunately this cannot be proved.

That Jesus had most of his interchanges during his public ministry with the Pharisees cannot be doubted. The rather significantly
close relationship that Jesus had with the Pharisees led to problems
in drawing lines of distinction.[41] These problems were intensified in
the Christian community as the growing temporal distance in the
Gospels testifies to the increasingly important role of the Pharisees.
The Pharisees were the Jewish movement that was closest to Christianity and with whom they were generally associated. To attempt
to conclude something about the actual significance of the Pharisees from this fact should be done only with great care. Luke seems
to have reckoned, most probably, on the possibility of achieving an
understanding between the two. Matthew and John, on the other
hand, regarded the two sides as hardening their respective positions.
Certainly, the intensified polemic against the Pharisees was connected with the suppression of the Jewish dimension in the Christian communities.[42]

3. RABBINIC STATEMENTS

3.1 Methodology

One usually begins with the assumption that the rabbinate was the
direct heir of the Pharisees after 70 C.E. and therefore that the New
Testament blends the situation of the decades after 70 with that of
the life of Jesus, focusing on the Pharisees as the implacable and
predominant enemies of Jesus. For that reason, however, many believe that we may accept rabbinic texts without further ado as direct

41. In Jewish literature on Jesus there is usually a direct relationship between
Jesus and the Pharisees. Thus B. A. Finkel, *The Pharisees*; H. Falk, *Jesus the
Pharisee* (New York, 1985). But see also R. A. Wild, *The Encounter,* 124: we
should not exclude the possibility "that Jesus himself was raised in the Pharisaic
tradition and so was a natural object of concern for his fellow sectarians."

42. U. Luz, *Jesus,* 232, correctly emphasizes the ambivalence of the New
Testament: Where the Christian community "stood in close proximity to historic
Judaism, the portrait of the Pharisees was negative and clearly tendentious. Where
the church and Judaism developed apart from each other, the picture was more
varied but also less clear."

testimony about the Pharisees and fill out our meager supply of information about the Pharisees with the rich rabbinic material. Even J. Neusner (whom no one would accuse of uncritical acceptance of rabbinic texts), at the time of the writing of his work *The Rabbinic Traditions about the Pharisees before 70,* without discussion of his criteria, treats all the traditions about precursors of the rabbinic movement in the rabbinic literature as Pharisaic.[43] We must ask the question explicitly: How can we prove such a continuity from the Pharisees to the rabbinic tradition? The personalities from the period before 70, selected by Neusner, are generally described in his own sources as *not* being Pharisees. In the case of Samias and Pollio, whom Josephus labels as Pharisees, Neusner finds the discussion of the extent to which we might identify these two with the rabbinic figures Shammai and Abtalion to be pointless.[44] Then, however, only Gamaliel I and Simeon ben Gamaliel are left, as people who are designated as Pharisees in the New Testament or Josephus. So primary a figure as Hillel is not mentioned before the rabbinic literature, and Johanan ben Zakkai only appears there. Was the leading role played by the family of Gamaliel sufficient both among the Pharisees and later in the rabbinate for an unbroken continuity of the two movements? Why do the rabbis not identify themselves as Pharisees? Why do they make such critical pronouncements about the Pharisees, so that even the identification of these *perušim* with the historical Pharisees is questionable? If this is supposed to be the same group, the name change would at least suggest that there were efforts toward a renewed identity (it might be that *Pharisee* was not a self-designation but a name given by outsiders).

The closing chapter of this work will discuss the question of the continuity of the Pharisees (before 70 C.E.) with the rabbis. Let it

43. J. Neusner, *Das pharisäische und talmudische Judentum* (Tübingen, 1984), 106: "The perception that the Mishnah scholars of the period before 70 might have been Pharisees is justified and even probable, if not proven thus far." In n. 20 he makes a significant retreat: Gamaliel and his son Simeon are identified as Pharisees; since they follow in the chains of tradition of *m. ʾAbot* 1 and *m. Hag.* 2.2, "it appears probable to me that the others in the chains were also Pharisees, but I grow increasingly less certain about this inference."

44. J. Neusner, *The Rabbinic Traditions* 1:159.

suffice here simply to acknowledge the problem without postulating a solution that will require proof. Thus, it seems to me that E. Rivkin's method is important, because he does not simply regard all of the rabbis of the period before 70 as Pharisees; he limits himself to those rabbinic texts that speak specifically of *perušin* and *ṣaddukin*—especially where the two are mentioned together—thus clarifying the question of whether these texts speak of the historic Pharisees and Sadducees, and perhaps whether there are prejudices behind the texts, and how they might be useful for a historic reconstruction.[45] As with the other groups of sources, we need to pay close attention to the temporal sequence of each document. The main accent will be on the Mishnah, and after it the texts from the Tosepta must be discussed, adding parallels from both Talmudim, but avoiding unnecessary repetitions. Finally, we have the Talmudic and other texts without earlier parallels. Our first step will be to separate out the very important texts often used to reconstruct the image of the Pharisees, which are, nevertheless, unusable.

3.2 Unusable and Questionable Texts

Not all rabbinic texts that speak of the *perušin* or *ṣaddukin* are useful for our study. The text-critical question is prominent with the *ṣaddukin*. Later manuscripts and printings use the word in place of *min*, 'aberrant, heretic,' which sensitive Christian censors applied to (Jewish) Christians.[46] The word *paruš* simply means 'separated' and can refer to various ascetic groups that had nothing to do with the Pharisees.

---

45. E. Rivkin, *A Hidden Revolution*, 125ff. (the chapter is almost the same as *HUCA* 40f., 1969f., 205-49). Also Lightstone, *Sadducees versus Pharisees,* is limited to this limited group of texts. For the remaining utilization of the rabbinic texts, I cannot agree with Rivkin when he, for example, automatically assumes the Pharisees as the opponents of the Sadducees, and thus also classifies Johanan ben Zakkai, the eldest of the court, the *Soferim,* or the anonymous rabbinic *halakah* with the Pharisees.

46. In the Mishnah there are three examples written over in the Albeck edition (*Para* 3.3; *Yad.* 4.8: *ṣadduki* twice in the singular), where the original text read *min*, likewise in *Ber.* 9.5 in the version of the usual Talmud printing.

The problem of utilizing texts about the *perušin* was already made clear in the Mishnah in *m. Hag.* 2.7. The text concerns the question of the laws of ritual purity (*midras* is a category of impurity transmitted by pressure without direct contact):

> For Pharisees the clothes of an ʿ*am ha-ʾareṣ* count as suffering *midras*-uncleanness; for them that eat Heave-offering the clothes of Pharisees count as suffering *midras*-uncleanness; for them that eat of Hallowed Things the clothes of them that eat Heave offering count as suffering *midras*-uncleanness; for them that occupy themselves with the Sin-offering water the clothes of them that eat of Hallowed Things count as suffering *midras*-uncleanness. Joseph b. Joezer was the most pious in the priesthood, yet for them that ate of Hallowed Things his apron counted as suffering *midras*-uncleanness. Johanan b. Gudgada always ate [his common food] in accordance with [the rules governing] the cleanness of Hallowed Things, yet for them that occupied themselves with the Sin-offering water his apron counted as suffering *midras*-uncleanness.

We are not concerned about particulars here. The important thing is the ranking of the *perušin* in the scale of ritual purity. They are on the second lowest rung, just above the ʿ*am ha-ʾareṣ*, the untrained people who were not concerned with the refinements of the law, but below the priestly families that are not in service, who are permitted to eat the food of the offering. The New Testament writes about the Pharisees' special efforts to observe the ordinances of ritual purity, thus maintaining distance from the tax collectors and sinners. In this context, however, we are not necessarily dealing with Pharisees, but just with people who keep themselves separate (*poršin*) from less observant people. Practical compliance with this classification by means of a scale of ritual purity at the time of the temple would have created a radical caste-like system separating people from each other, and it is hardly conceivable. Likewise the understanding of *m. Soṭa* 3.4 regarding the Pharisees is questionable:

> R. Eliezer says: If any man gives his daughter a knowledge of the Law it is as though he taught her lechery. R. Joshua says: A woman has more pleasure in one *kab* [a measure of volume] than in nine

kabs with modesty (*perišut*). He used to say: A foolish saint and a cunning knave and a woman that is a hypocrite (*isha peruša*) and the wounds of the Pharisees (*perušin*), these wear out the world.

Like many others, H. Bietenhard associated this with the Pharisees; he translates "a Pharisee woman, the blows of the Pharisees" and sees this as a parallel of the New Testamant polemic against the Pharisees.[47] Nevertheless, this is probably spoken generally in regard to people who regard themselves as pious, and for that reason they separate themselves from ordinary people. We will have to wait to see other passages for a more direct association with the Pharisees.

The Tosepta also speaks frequently about *perušin* whose identification with the Pharisees is either questionable or completely impossible. *T. Šabb.* 1.15 (Lieberman 4; *y. Šabb.* 1.5.3c) connects with the assertion of *m. Šabb.* 1.3 that the observation of laws of ritual purity were so thorough that no man who has a genital discharge (*zab*) may eat with a woman who is similarly afflicted (*zabah*), not because it is forbidden, because it could lead to a trangression,

> For the house of Shammai says, "A *zab paruš* should not eat with a *zab* who is an ʿ*am ha-ʾareṣ*. Nevertheless, the house of Hillel permits it."

It might be that we ought to interpret *zab paruš* as a Pharisee with such an affliction.[48] If this person does not otherwise eat with a man of the common people because he is afraid that he might be rendered unclean, he ought not to do so here. Otherwise he might grow accustomed to neglecting the law.

On the other hand, E. Rivkin would interpret *paruš* here as a man who is praised for maintaining a certain degree of ritual purity, implying a separation from the ʿ*am ha-ʾareṣ* and thus one who is voluntarily separated. His justification that Pharisees stood in contrast to Sadducees or Boethusians, but not to the common people, is

47. H. Bietenhard, *Sota* ["Giessener Mischna"] (Berlin, 1956), 72f.
48. Thus translated by J. Neusner, *The Tosefta: Moed* (New York, 1981), 3: "A *zab* who is a Pharisee should not eat with a *zab* who is of common folk."

problematic and needs to be tested, even if the text quoted above, *m. Hag.* 2.7, with its graduation of ʿam ha-ʾareṣ/perušin, is comparable. In contrast, Rivkin's reference to the singular *paruš* instead of the plural in the clearly Pharisaic passages has merit.[49] The interpretation of Lev. 11:44 in *Sifra Shemini* 12:4 (Weiss 57b) is also interesting: "As holy as I am, so holy ought you to be; as I am *parush*, so you ought to be *perušin*" (we find the same interpretation for 19:2 in *Sifra Qedoshim* 1, Weiss 86c); in *Mekhilta Baḥodeš* 2 (Lauterbach 2:206) for Exod. 19:6, he interprets "holy people" as "separated (*perušin*) from the people of the world and their horrors." It would be attractive to use the *Sifra* text to support the idea that the Pharisees regarded themselves as "holy ones"; nevertheless, the context shows that the text is about the separation of Israel as a whole. It is by this separation that God sanctifies his own. The passage is not about the separation of the Pharisees from the ʿam ha-ʾareṣ.

T. Sota 15.11-12 (Lieberman 242f.; similar *B.Bat.* 60b) states that after the destruction of the Temple there were many *perušin* in Israel who would not eat meat or drink wine because of their grief. The rabbis rejected this as an extreme reaction. The *perušin* here are clearly not Pharisees but people who set themselves apart from certain pleasures: ascetics. Likewise, the following text clearly does not speak about Pharisees. According to it, the petitions of the eighteen prayers correspond to the eighteen times God's name is mentioned in Psalm 29, and from there additional petitions are added to others to keep that number.

> One adds the [benediction] of the minim to that of the *perušin*, that of the proselytes to that of the elders, and those about David in [the text] "the one who builds Jerusalem" (*t. Ber.* 3.25, Lieberman 18).

In this passage *perušin* can only be analogous to *minim*, thus "one who deviates, a heretic." These are people who are separated from the community of Israel. In *y. Ber.* 2.4.8a, in place of *perušin* we find "blasphemer" (*rešaim*, similar 4.3.8a: *pošʿim*).

---

49. E. Rivkin, *A Hidden Revolution*, 171.

Finally, there is the frequently found list of the seven kinds of *perušin*, which are at least of questionable use to complete a picture of the Pharisees. The earliest citation is found in ʾ*Abot de Rabbi Nathan* B 45 (Schechter 124) and A 37 (Schechter 109). The variations in the designation in the manuscript tradition and in contrast to the Talmudic evidence shows how difficult a few of the expressions were even in early times. It is therefore sensible to proceed with a version with commentary, namely, that of *y. Ber.* 9.7.14b (almost identical to *y. Sota* 5.7.20a):

> There are seven [kinds of] *perušin*: There is a shoulder *paruš*, a *paruš niqpi* [circumstantial, protracted?], a calculating *paruš*, a miserly *paruš*, a *paruš* who says "I would like to know my duty, then I will do it," a *paruš* of fear, a *paruš* of love.
>
> 1. A shoulder *paruš* carries the commandments on his shoulder.
> 2. A circumstantial *paruš* says "Wait for me; I want to keep a commandment."
> 3. A calculating *paruš* commits a sin and fulfils a commandment [compensating for one with the other].
> 4. A miserly *paruš* [says] "I take from what I have to fulfill a commandment."
> 5. A *paruš* "I would like to know my duty, then I will do it," "what guilt have I incurred that I might fulfill a corresponding commandment?"
> 6. A *paruš* of fear like Job.
> 7. A *paruš* of love like Abraham.
>
> None of them is worth more for you than a *paruš* of love like Abraham.

This paragraph was added to both versions of the Palestinian Talmud between statements about Job and Abraham. Despite the usual articulation of different types of Pharisees, here the use of the singular indicates that we should be careful. There is no instance in the rabbinic literature where *paruš* in the singular clearly refers to a Pharisee. The meaning 'holy one' or 'pious one' here as in the previously mentioned passages is entirely possible and probable. Therefore, the text offers a graduated scale of piety, beginning with

demonstrative fulfillment of commandments, through rather mathe-
matical thinking, all the way to the level that is based in the fear of
God. The high point is the holiness that proceeds from completely
selfless love. Job and Abraham are the biblical examples of that
highest degree of holiness, not the unflatteringly regarded Pharisee.
The text of *b. Sota* 22b introduces the list at least as *abaraita*. In
contrast to the parallels in the Palestinian Talmud, *m. Sota* 3.4 comments on the moderate woman (*iša perušah*) and the blows of the
pious (*perušin*) that destroy the world and is thus understood in a
completely negative manner. Statements about women that are too
pious and students who pretend to teach *halakah* too quickly come
first. The demand to strike the *paruš* from the list for reasons of
love and fear follows the list and its commentary. This also argues
against the idea of a list of Pharisees: would the rabbis, who were
seen as successors of the Pharisees, have had reason not to find any
positive form of Pharisee?

The text continues completely without parallel:

> King Jannaeus said to his wife: "Don't be afraid of the *perušin* or of
> those who are not *perushin* but rather of the hypocrites who imitate
> *perushin* whose works resemble those of Zimri and who desire the
> reward of Pinhas." (*b. Sota* 22b)

We might interpret the passage that neither religious nor irreli-
gious elements were a danger to the authorities, but rather those
who arrange religion to suit their own purposes. Nevertheless, we
probably ought to remember Josephus's report here, according to
which the dying Alexander Jannaeus suggested a reconciliation with
the Pharisees, since they would be able to cause much harm (*AJ*
13.401f.). That would mean that at the latest, the redactor who had
added this piece had connected the list with the Pharisees, a misunderstanding that later became commonplace because of the addition.

3.3 The Mishnah

Only one text in the Mishnah mentions the *perušin* together with
the *ṣaddukin,* for which an interpretation here of Pharisees and
Sadducees is assured. It is *m. Yad.* 4.6-8, a stylistically complete
textual unity. First, 4.6 is concerned with the Holy Scripture:

The Sadducees say, We cry out against you, O ye Pharisees, for ye say, "The Holy Scriptures render the hands unclean," [and] the writings of Hamiram [Homer] do not render the hands unclean. Rabban Johanan b. Zakkai said, Have we naught against the Pharisees save this!—for lo, they say, "the bones of an ass are clean, and the bones of Johanan the High Priest are unclean." They said to him, As is our love for them so is their uncleanness—that no man make spoons of the bones of his father or mother. He said to them, Even so the Holy Scriptures: as is our love for them so is their uncleanness; [whereas] the writings of Hamiram which are held in no account do not render the hands unclean.

First, it is remarkable that Johanan ben Zakkai counts himself (merely rhetorically?) among the opposition to the Pharisees, according to the answer of the Sadducees(?), but with the Sadducees he justifies the Pharisees' position and thus closes the debate. That which sounds abnormal in the pronouncement on the Holy Scripture corresponds wholly to the Pharisaic pronouncement on corpses. To what degree this mirrors an actual disagreement between Pharisees and Sadducees is very doubtful. The text rather gives us an impression of justifying rabbinic conceptual development in the form of a disagreement with the Sadducees. Concerning the tone of the discussion, J. Lightstone opines, "The only purpose served is the vilification of the Sadducees."[50] In reality, however, there is no degradation of the opponent; the tone is very moderate.

The first part of *m. Yad.* 4.7 is constructed formally in the same manner; in the second part the content of the complaint is missing, which the later Mishnah amplifies.

The Sadducees say, We cry out against you, O ye Pharisees, for you declare clean an unbroken stream of liquid [*niṣoq* the pure discharge that flows in an impure person]. The Pharisees say, We cry out against you, O ye Sadducees, for ye declare clean a channel of water that flows from a burial ground. The Sadducees say, We cry out against you, O ye Pharisees, for ye say, "If my ox or my ass have done an injury they are culpable, but if my bondman or my bond-

50. J. Lightstone, *Sadducees*, 208.

woman have done an injury they are not culpable"—if in the case of my ox or my ass (about which no commandments are laid upon me) I am responsible for the injury that they do, how much more in the case of my bondman or my bondwoman (about whom certain commandments are laid upon me) must I be responsible for the injury that they do! They say to them, No!—as ye argue concerning my ox or my ass (which have no understanding) would ye likewise argue concerning my bondman or my bondwoman which have understanding?—for if I provoke him to anger he may go and set fire to another's stack of corn, and it is I that must make restitution!

The first confrontation of the Sadducees and the Pharisees here again concerns decisions in matters of ritual purity that seem inconsequential. Details of the exposition of the text (especially the interpretation of *nitsoq* and the question of the admissability of a flow of water from a cemetery) are highly controversial.[51] The only essential thing here is the assertion that the stricter understanding of the text was at one time held by the Sadducees and at another by the Pharisees. The Sadducees were not accused of religious laxity, but only of a different position.

The second disagreement concerns civil law. The Sadducees declared an owner responsible for the injury caused by his cattle, and even more so when caused by his slaves (he even had special religious concerns for slaves, especially the obligation to circumcise). The Pharisees (corresponding to the Mishnah emphasis on intention) rejected this with an appeal to everyone's personal responsibility.

M. Yad. 4.8 maintains this same basic form, yet it is now a Galilean *min*[52] that complains about the Pharisees and their practice

---

51. For a partially farfetched, metaphorical explanation, see G. Lisowsky in the "Giessener Mischna" (Jadajim, 1956), 76f.; J. Patrich, *A Sadducean Halakha,* 26f. Patrich connnects this decision (made by a Sadducean Sanhedrin and consequently ascribed to the Sadducees, even if the rabbinic *halakah* agrees) with the construction of the aqueduct to the Temple during the Hasmonean period. Excavations have shown that it actually did go through a cemetery.

52. M. Hengel, *The Zealots,* 58f., is thinking here with H. Graetz of disciples of the Galilean Judas, and thus zealots.

in documents of dating according to the rulers. Then follow the Pharisees' countercharges. It is not only that the *min* has been replaced by a Sadducee in later copies, the remaining text is also in disarray. It is remarkable that the text concludes the argumentation with Exod. 9:27: "The Lord is in the right (*ṣaddik*)." Maimonides regarded this as an insertion, which was intended to conclude the text in a positive manner. Could we not rather see this as the concluding encounter with the *ṣaddikin*? They designate themselves as *ṣaddikin*, but in reality only God is a *ṣaddik*. This might be an attack upon the Sadducees' opinion of themselves, but it remains very measured and implied.

In general, *m. Yad.* 4.6-8 works like a preformed unity that only secondarily was added to the corpus of the tractate. In substance, the text, which summarizes the points of disagreement between the Pharisees and the Sadducees, is not unified, even if the theme of ritual purity dominates. Pharisees, like Sadducees, are designated as a group that is very interested in questions of ritual purity. They differ from each other in particulars, but it is hard to establish a principal behind the differences. Even the motive behind a master's responsibility is not clear.[53] The Sadducees may defend their position, even if the Pharisees always get the last word and win the argument. The Mishnah is clearly on the side of the Pharisees, and in this single text, which certainly speaks about the Pharisees, seems to equate the rabbinic position with that of the Pharisees. Yet this still does not mean that it identifies the rabbis with the Pharisees.

Sadducees are mentioned frequently. As in *m. Yad.* 4, in *m. Para* 3.7f. questions of ritual purity are being treated. In the "Rite of the Red Heifer" the Pharisees desire greater purity of the priest than the official ritual.

53. When L. Finkelstein, *The Pharisees,* sees the interests of the possessing class represented by the Sadducees and the humanistic side represented by the Pharisees, that does not cover this text. It is indeed the Sadducees who emphasize arrest by the employer! Finkelstein's social-historical discussion overextends the bounds of the text.

And the elders of Israel used to go forth before them on foot to the Mount of Olives. There was a place of immersion there; and they had [first] rendered unclean the priest that should burn the Heifer because of the Sadducees: that they should be able to say, "It must be performed by them on who the sun has set."

They laid their hands on him and said, "My Lord the High Priest, immrse thyself this once." He went down and immersed himself and came up and dried himself.

The text does not say whether the priest here was a Sadducee or not. It presupposes that the "elders of Israel" were not Sadducees, in contrast to the current view of the assembling of the Sanhedrin before 70 C.E. In so doing it follows the general rabbinic interpretation. The priest was required to observe the strictest prescriptions regarding ritual purity. Historically it is, of course, completely unthinkable that he would then, in the context of the rite, become unclean simply to demonstrate the correctness of a particular interpretation of the laws of purity.[54]

Thus the text is polemical, but extremely measured in tone if we compare it with parallel passages in the Tosepta. The same is true of *m. Nid.* 4.2, which again deals with laws for ritual purity, especially rules for the treatment of menstruating women.

The only two texts from the Mishnah on the Sadducees outside the order of the Toharot are found in *m. ʿErub.* 6.2 and *m. Mak.* 1.6. The first text (see p. 74 below) treats a rather narrowly defined distinction regarding the ʿerub, the mixing of private and public arenas in questions of Sabbath rest. The second case (see p. 87 below) concerns the time of execution of false witnesses in a capital trial. According to the opinion of the Sadducees, they are to be executed immediately upon condemnation; in the view of the sages, only after the innocent party has been executed. The Sadducees are portrayed in this text as opponents who are easy to refute; naturally,

---

54. The interpretation in V. Epstein, "When and how the Sadducees were excommunicated," *JBL* 85 (1966): 213–24, is quite imaginative. He would deduce the excommunication of the Sadducees by Johanan ben Zakkai around 60/61 C.E. from this and other rabbinic citations.

the rabbinic opinion wins out, yet without this being connected with negative remarks about the Sadducees.

M. Menaḥ. 10.3 is also the only place in the Mishnah that mentions the Boethusians, by which we usually understand the family and followers of the high priest Boethus. The complex rite for the cutting of the first barley sheaf just after the first feast day of Passover is supposed to parry a different dating of the ceremony by the Boethusians. Here also, the demonstrative enforcement of their own point of view (not designated as Pharisaic) is not connected with direct polemic against the Boethusians.

In summary, we may assert that the Mishnah speaks of Pharisees much more often than Sadducees, who appear in only one text unit. The Mishnah ascribes to the Sadducees nine *halakic* positions and contrasts them on five cases (four of them on issues of ritual purity) with those of the Pharisees. Six of the Sadducean positions concern laws regarding ritual purity, each concerning the Sabbath and civil law, as well as criminal law. The dominance of issues of ritual purity mirrors primarily the interests of the rabbis, perhaps also of the Pharisees who at this very point drew a line of separation between themselves and the Sadducees. We do not know whether this area was also of central concern for the Sadducees. This might be possible if we could regard the Sadducees who held the dominant point of view primarily as a party of the priestly nobility. At most, one text in the Mishnah (*Para*) suggests a Sadducean (high) priest.

How can we explain the infrequent appearance of the Pharisees in the Mishnah, if the rabbis are supposed to be the successors of the Pharisaic movement? We might argue that the term was expressly avoided, and the rabbis, even where they regard themselves as successors of the Pharisees, prefer expressions like *soferim, ḥakamim,* or *ḥaberim* as a group designation or simply mention the name of a representative of a particular *halakah*. Even if a part of this interpretation might be correct, the uncontrolled, general application would, nevertheless, be a *petitio principii*—a circular argument that is useless for historical analysis.

3.4 Tosepta and Parallels

The Tosepta mentions the Sadducees only three times, and always in the context of matters of ritual purity. Nevertheless, texts can be included that mention the Boethusians, because they replace the Sadducees frequently in Mishnah parallels. Apparently they were equated with the Sadducees or at least were regarded as a branch of them.

At the beginning, the only text that connects the Pharisees and the Sadducees should be mentioned: *t. Chag.* 3.35 (L. 394):

> M'SH: They immersed the candelabrum on the festival day, and Sadducees went around saying, "Come and see how the Pharisees immerse [something as clean as] the light of the moon."

The Mishnah parallel passage (*m.* ®*ag.* 3.8) speaks of the purification of the Temple court yard, and warns against touching the (show bread) table and the lamps and rendering them unclean. When they had to clean the table, they placed no show bread on it until the next Sabbath. The menorah also had to burn constantly. The Mishnah says that there were enough utensils for two or three duplicate sets, in case of an accident. That also appears to have included the menorah. The warning about its being unclean would then be based on the circumstances of an exchange. The Tosepta text apparently illustrates this warning with a list of examples. The heart of the text is the view that the Sadducees thought that the menorah could not be made unclean (as assumed by the rabbis in regard to the golden and the copper altar.) No reason is given for this. Apart from the probably fictive situation, the text adds the image commanded by the Mishnah, according to which the Sadducees have a partially differing law regarding ritual purity. It is noteworthy that there is no direct criticism of the Pharisees. Apparently we are able to interpret the sentence in a positive manner, so that it even fits with the closing words of the tractate. In that passage the Sadducees have the last word in their criticism of the Pharisees.

T. Yad. 2.19f. (Rengstorf 360) corresponds to the disagreement between the Sadducees (here Boethusians) and the Pharisees in *m. Yad.* 4.6-8:

> A. Said to them Rabban Yoḥanan b. Zakkai, "The preciousness of Holy Scriptures accounts for their uncleanness,
>
> B. "so that a man should not make them into bedding for his cattle."

A. The Boethusians say, "We complain against you, Pharisees.

B. "Now if the daughter of my son, who inherits on the strength of my son, who inherits on my account, lo, she inherits me—my daughter, who comes on my account [directly], logically should inherit me."

C. Say Pharisees, "No. If you have said so in regard to the daughter of the son, who shares with the brothers, will you say so of the daughter, who does not share with the brothers?"

D. Those who immerse at dawn say, "We complain against you, Pharisees.

E. "For you mention the divine nature at dawn without first immersing."

F. Say Pharisees, "We complain against you, those who immerse at dawn.

G. "For you make mention of the divine name in a body which contains uncleanness."

The text functions as a variation of the Mishnah text, summarizing a developed state of affairs and completing other things that are only suggested. Here, as there, in the midst of the uniformity we find a theme from civil law: in the Mishnah the question of responsibility for harm committed by slaves, and in the Tosepta a question of inheritance. The beginning of the Tosepta text requires the Mishnah for comprehension. As there, here also the Pharisees are victorious in the disagreement. The Boethusians may have briefly advanced their argument, but the Pharisees have the last word. The tone, however, remains extremely objective. This is all the more remarkable when one sees how the Tosepta, otherwise frequently concerned with Sadducees and Boethusians, here has only mockery and scorn for them.

The middle section, on the rights of a daughter to be an heir, is found in *y. B. Bat.* 8.1.1a, but here the Boethusians replace the Pharisees. By contrast, *B. Bat.* 115b-116a is of greatest interest. Here it first states that a person does not obey even a prince in Israel if he allows a daughter together with the daughter of a son to be heirs, because that would be the practice of the Sadducees. That is supported with the *baraita:* "On the 24th of Tebet we returned to our right" (thus *Megillat Taanit* for the 24th of Ab). Whether also the following, a historicization of the variation of opinions in the Tosepta, still ought to be regarded as a *baraita* is not clear.

> For the Pharisee used to say, "The daughter may inherit with the daughter of the son."
> Johanan ben Zakkai concerned himself with those things. He said to them, "You fools! Where do you get that?" And no one answered him, besides a certain old man who stammered before him and said, "If already the daughter of his son, who came from the power of his son, can be his heir, how much more his own daugher, who comes from his own power!" [Johanan] quoted the following Bible verse against him, "These are the sons of Seir the Horite . . ." [Gen. 36:20, the argumentation is not clear.]
> [The old man] said to him, "Rabbi, do you finish with me in this way?"
> [Johanan] answered him, "Fool! Isn't our perfect Torah as convincing as your futile palaver? The daughter of a son also has a right of inheritance where there are brothers. And you want to compare her with his [own] daughter, who has no right of inheritance, where there are brothers?"
> And he vanquished them. And they made this day a holiday.

It is difficult to say whether the conflicting notions regarding the right of inheritance in this text are to be viewed as historical. I would like to think that the quotation from *Megillat Taanit* (Scroll of Faith) was misunderstood, reduced to a single detail and combined with the issue of inheritance from *t. Yad.* Johanan ben Zakkai also emerges from that summary as the victorious speaker. The story simply molds into a narrative form the fact that the rabbinic view prevailed. It used the occasion to make fun of the Sadducees' lack of knowledge: they could not base their position in Scripture.

T. Men. 10.23 (Lieberman 528) picks up on *m. Men.* 10.3, the only text in the Mishnah that speaks of Boethusians instead of Sadducees, and adopts it almost word for word: directly after the end of the first day of Passover, a person goes into the field in order to cut a sheaf of barley, even if it is the Sabbath. At each point in the activity he asks the bystanders for their assent: "Why all this?

Because of the Boethusians who used to say, 'The cutting of the barley does not take place on the first day of the festival.'" The point at issue is so important because they counted the fifty days to the Festival of Weeks (thus the entire festival calendar) from the offering of the sheaf of barley.

The Mishnah and Tosepta, which are only concerned with expressing their own opinion and give the Boethusians marginal recognition, were first completed in the Babylonian Talmud, and again with a story in which Johanan ben Zakkai played the principal role. The commentary on the Mishnah employs a quote from the *Scroll of Fasts:*

> A person may not fast from the first until the eighth of Nisan, for the daily sacrifice (again) was employed at this time, likewise from the eighth of Nisan through the end of the feast, because of the (re)institution of the (date of the) Festival of Weeks.

The Gemara relates the first statement to the victory over the Sadducees, who deduced from the singular in Num. 28:4 that an individual may establish the daily sacrifice voluntarily. On the other hand, it was enforced (on the basis of the plural in 28:3) that this was paid for from the Temple treasury. Then follows the commentary on the question of dating:

> The Boethusians used to say, "The Festival of Weeks [ʿAṣeret] occurs [on the day] after the sabbath."
>
> Johanan ben Zakkai was engaged with them. He said to them, "You fools! Where did you get that?" And no one answered him anything, except an old man who stammered before him and said, "Moses, our teacher, loved Israel. And since he knew that the Festival of Weeks lasted only one day, he arose and established it on the sabbath so that Israel might enjoy two days."
>
> [Johanan] quoted this Bible verse against him, "'By the way of Mt. Seir it takes eleven days to reach Kadesh Barnea from Horeb' [Deut 1:2] and if Moses, our teacher, loved Israel, why did he hold them back for 40 years in the wilderness."
>
> [The old man] said to him, "Do you finish with me in this manner?"

[Johanan] answered him, "Fool! Isn't our perfect Torah [as convincing as] your futile palaver? A Bible passage states 'count fifty days' [Lev. 23:16] and another Bible passage says 'It ought to be seven full weeks' [23:15]."

How can that be? One text speaks of the feast day that occurs on the sabbath, and the other of a feast day that occurs in the middle of the week." (b. Men. 65a-b)

It is thus clarified from the rabbinic point of view that the Festival of Weeks may take place on any day of the week. In our study, the kind of legend development around Johanan ben Zakkai is essential. It was apparently copied mechanically from b. B. Bat. 115b-116a. The name of Johanan was given there in the Mishnah and Tosepta, and here it was simply added by analogy (as in b. B. Bat. in association with a quote from the Scroll of Fasts). In both places the Boethusians were made laughable and portrayed as being unable to support their views from the Bible.

The pleasure that is taken in the Tosepta in narration is brought to bear in the following episode in which a dispute over the calendar likewise stands at the center. M. Roš Haš. 2.1 states about the certification of the new moon, "In the beginning people accepted the witness of the new moon from anyone. Once the minim ruined things (misheqilqelu ha-minim), they decided to accept the information only from acquaintances." The Tosepta Roš Haš. 1.15 (Lieberman 308f.) quotes the Mishnah, replacing the colorless statement about the minim with a story:

In the beginning people used to accept evidence of the new moon from anyone.

Once the Boethusians bribed two witnesses to come and to lead the wise men into error, for the Boethusians desired that ʿAṣeret should always occur [on the day] after the sabbath. One came and put aside his testimony and went away.

The second one came and said, "I came upon the creature and saw him cowering between two rocks. His head resembled a calf, his ears a ram, his horns a stag and his tail was between his thighs. Amazed, I looked at him and fell back. And behold, there were 200 Zuz wrapped in my handkerchief."

They said to him, "The 200 Zuz were entrusted to you as a gift, nevertheless, the one who bribed you will be released to the pillars. What would you like to do?"

He said to them, "I have heard that the Boethusians wanted to lead the wise men astray. Then I said, 'Good, I will go and inform the wise men.'"

This story of the deceived deceiver is characteristic of the kind that the Tosepta and often the Mishnah tell. The only *fundamentum in re* may be to remember that there were disagreements over the date of the Festival of Weeks. The parallel *y. Roš Haš.* 3.57d-58a is nearly identical. *B. Roš Haš.* 22b introduces the story as a *baraita* and adds nearly from the beginning that the Boethusians bribed two witnesses with 400 zuz, "one of ours and one of theirs." The witness on the side of the Boethusians denied his testimony, while the other, who was on the side of the wise men, finished his unbelievable story with the words, "And if you don't believe me, look: 200 zuz are wrapped in my handkerchief." The text basically explicates his report without making substantive changes.

In other places the Tosepta incoporates Johanan ben Zakkai in his form as narrator and makes him into a victorious opponent of the Sadducees. *T. Para* 3.6f (Rengstorf 192) quotes, expands, and personalizes the previously cited Mishnah text:

Because of the Sadducees they maintained the priest to become unclean who burned the heifer, so that they might not say: It was prepared by [priests, who after the bath] who have waited for sundown.

And [there was] an occasion with a certain Sadducee who had waited for sundown and [then] came to burn the cow. And Rabbi Jochanan ben Zakkai learned about it and came and laid both hands on him and said to him, "My Lord, High Priest, as a high priest you are something! Get down and bathe again!"

He got down, bathed again and came out.

After he had come out, grabbed him [Johanan] by the ear and said, "Ben Zakkai, wait until I am free!"

This one answered him, "Until you are free!"

It was not even three days before he was laid in his grave. His father came to Rabbi Johanan ben Zakkai and said to him, "Ben Zakkai, my son has not been free."

The text is probably only to be interpreted as a legendary reformation of the Mishnah. Johanan ben Zakkai replaces the elders; a Sadducee replaces a priest not further identified in the Mishnah. There is only scorn for the uncleanness of the priest. It is not clear whether ben Zakkai yanked the high priest by the ear, making him unfit for cultic activity (compare *m. Bek.* 5.3 for this interpretation of the expression), or simply pulled him by the ear, or whether the high priest did this to Johanan. The first possibility fits well with the burlesque described here. Nothing further is said regarding the completion of the rite. Johanan ben Zakkai can humiliate the priest in his function here with impunity. If he were to threaten him because of it, the consequence would be the death of the high priest. This is a comically overdrawn scene in which even Johanan ben Zakkai is not a religious model.

According to *m. Yoma* 1.5 the elders of the court instruct the high priest before the Day of Atonement how he ought to complete his rites, making him swear that he will not change anything. Then "he went away crying, and they went away crying." *T. Yoma* 1.8 (Lieberman 222f.) comments on this Mishnah text.

Why did he go away crying? Because it was necessary for him to swear.

Why did they go away crying? Because they had to swear.

And why did they make him swear?

There was once a case with a certain Boethusian who prepared the incense while he was still outside [the holy of holies]. And the cloud of incense spread and the whole house trembled.

For the Boethusians used to say,

"He ought to burn incense while he is still outside, for it is said,

"That the cloud of the incense may cover the mercy seat that is upon the covenant, or he will die." [Lev. 16:13]

The wise men said to him, "Does it not also say, 'he ought to light the incense before the Lord. [Lev. 16:13] Thus anyone who lights incense should do it only after he is inside.

"If that is so, why does it say then, 'that the cloud of incense may cover?'"

"That teaches that he gives something that allows the incense to climb up. For he did nothing to allow the incense to climb up, he would be guilty of death."

When [the Boethusian] came out, he said to his father, "All of your days you have arranged and [afterward] not touched anything, until I arose and handled."

He said to him, "Even though we made arrangements [in this manner], we did not handle [afterward, for] we obeyed the words of the wise men. I would not be surprised if you were to live a long time."

It was not three days before they laid him in his grave.

The story is comparable to that of *t. Para* 3.6f., except that the high priest here is not a Sadducee but a Boethusian. The exposition of Lev. 16:13 by the wise men (Pharisees are not mentioned) is appropriate, since the Boethusians were rather practically oriented. Since the mere sight of the mercy seat was deadly, they had to cover it from the outset with incense. For that reason the incense was lighted while still outside, instead of relying on some method of lighting incense on the inside. We might interpret this in such a way that the exposition of the verse ascribed to the Boethusians actually determined the cultic action, while the rabbis read from the Bible that it actually had to be different.[55] We can gather from the discussion of *m. Yoma* 5.1, regarding whether there were one or two curtains in front of the holy of holies that their knowledge of the proceedings was not very precise. This corresponds to the tendency of the Tosepta to clothe theoretical discussion in a factual story in which the view of the rabbis naturally states the will of God.

The parallel *y. Yoma* 1.5.39 includes this same story without biblical support; nevertheless, it describes the death of the high-handed priest.

---

55. The parallel *Sifra Ahare* 3.11 (Weiss 81b) does not contain this story, but only the disagreement with the Sadducees about the interpretation of Leviticus 16. This was taken as a self-contained unit also in *y. Yoma* 1.5.39a-b and *b. Yoma* 53a. Philo described the rite in the same way as attributed to the Boethusians here (*Spec. leg.* 1.72.).

They say, "There were no easy days before he died." And many said, "Worms came out of his nose, and something like the hoof of a calf came out of his forehead."

The motif of the worms marks the priest as a blasphemer (see, for example, 2 Macc. 9:9 on the death of Antiochus IV); the calf's hoof is, of course, the footprint of one of the four creatures that carry the throne of God, and it kicks against the sinner. *B. Yoma* 19b offers the same story, introduced as a *baraita*, but takes it further; the text speaks of Sadducees, not Boethusians. The high priest comes full of joy from the holy of holies, but his father says to him, "My son, even though we are Sadducees, we fear the Pharisees." Here for the first time, in contrast to the parallels, the Pharisees are introduced. The statement of the earlier texts that they listened to the interpretation of the wise men and then acted exaggerates the Sadducees' fear of the Pharisees. This motif appears in the Babylonian Talmud frequently and points to later interests, in spite of the introduction as a *baraita*. Even the description of the death of the blasphemer is expanded further: he dies after a few days, his body is thrown on the garbage heap, and worms crawl from his nose. According to other opinions he was struck down as he left the holy of holies, and a kind of voice was heard in the Temple court as though an angel came from heaven and struck him in the face. The priests who found him decided that something like a calf's foot was between his shoulders, corresponding to the description of the being in Ezek. 1:7. Despite the claim of a *baraita* the narrator invents his tale freely in the interest of his propaganda.

In comparison with the preceding, two narratives from the Tosepta are harmless. According to them the Boethusians did not respect certain folk rites during the Feast of Tabernacles. *M. Sukk.* 4.6 establishes that the people go in procession around the altar, striking the ground with willow rods on the sixth day of the festival (or the seventh day when it falls on a Sabbath.) According to *t. Sukk.* 3.1 (Lieberman 266) the Boethusians, according to whom this rite is not permitted on the Sabbath, covered the willow branches prepared for the event with great stones. The people noticed it, however, and took them out again (likewise *b. Sukk.* 43b).

T. Sukk. 3.16 (Lieberman 270f.) is related to the cited passage. The Mishnah *Sukk.* 4.9 says about the libation on the altar prescribed at the Feast of Tabernacles, "To the priest who performed the libation they used to say, 'Lift up thine hand!' for once a certain one poured the libation over his feet, and all the people threw their citrons at him."

Most often this text is connected with the story about Alexander Jannaeus (*AJ* 13.372), where the libation is not mentioned. The Tosepta expands this brief note:

C. For there already was the case of the *Boethusian who poured out the water on his feet, and all the people stoned him with their citrons* [M. Suk. 4:9N-O].

D. And the horn of the altar was damaged, so the sacred service was cancelled for that day, until they brought a lump of salt and put it on it, so that the altar should not appear to be damaged.

E. For any altar lacking a horn, ramp, or foundation is invalid.

Here also the Tosepta identifies the priest as a Boethusian. He is apparently not acquainted with this rite of the libation (not biblically attested). We also find that the altar was damaged in the ensuing tumult in *y. Yoma* 1.5.39a and *y. Sukk.* 4.8.54d, where, however, the episodes of the Day of Atonement and of the Feast of Tabernacles are mixed together. Historically, it is difficult to evaluate this embroidering of the simple observation in the Talmud. Even the inclusion of the Boethusian may come from the general tendency of the Tosepta toward concretization. *B. Sukk.* 48b has taken over the narrative, except that it replaced the Boethusian with a Sadducee.

T. Nid. 5.2f (Rengstorf 235) first quotes the Mishnah and illustrates it with a story. The text with its Mishnah citation resembles the previously mentioned pieces:

A. Sadducean women, when they are accustomed to follow in the ways of their fathers, lo, they are like Samaritans.

B. [If] they left [those ways to walk] in the ways of Israel, lo, they are like Israel[ites].[45]

A. M'ŚH B: A Sadducean chatted with a high priest, and spit

spurted from his mouth and fell on the garments of the high priest, and the face of the high priest blanched.

B. Then he came and asked his [the Sadducee's] wife, and she said, "My lord priest: Even though we are Sadducean women, they [we] all bring their inquiries to a sage."

C. Said R. Yosé, "We are more expert in the Sadducean women than anyone. For they all bring their questions to a sage, except for one who was among them, and she died."

In contrast to the previous narratives from the Tosepta concerning priests and the cult, this text presupposes that the high priest is not a Sadducee and thus fears the saliva of a Sadducee, who together with his wife perhaps does not observe all of the prescriptions regarding ritual purity during her period and are unclean.[56] Nevertheless, the Sadducean woman assured him that she was guided by all the rabbinic scholars ("wise men") and thus followed the path of Israel. So also here the rabbinic interpretation is completely victorious, and death punishes the only woman who had contradicted that interpretation. Thus rabbinic wishful thinking influenced this text also. *B. Nid.* 33b includes this story almost word for word as a *baraita*. The woman's answer to the high priest is formulated in a manner corresponding to the text already quoted in *b. Yoma* 19b: "Even though they are Sadducean women, they fear the Pharisees" and have their blood tested by their wise men.

The Talmud then comments that a Sadducee is not comparable to an ʿam ha-ʾareṣ, by whom one cannot in principle be made unclean during a festival—a decision made out of necessity and required to make the course of a festival with popular participation at all possible—but a *ḥaber* is such a one (earlier there is even a discussion of a Samaritan *ḥaber!*), that is, someone who is obligated to be especially precise in matters of tithing and ritual purity and whose un-

56. Numerous parallels (*y. Meg.* 1.12.72a; *y. Hor.* 3.5.47d; *LevR* 20.11, Margulies 470; and so on) tell the story of the high priest who became unclean and consequently unfit for service before the Day of Atonement because of the saliva of an Arabian king (thus a heathen whose saliva was especially unclean). Perhaps the story was secondarily associated with a Sadducee.

cleanness must therefore be considered even on feast days. Even the (late) statement was made out of concern for the consistent nature of the legal system; it shows, nevertheless, that the rabbis also approved of a Sadducee's serious efforts toward an exact observation of the law.

T. Sanh. 6.6 (Zuckermandel 424) takes up the theme of the false witnesses from *Mak.* I.6, according to which they are to be punished when the innocent party is found guilty and not only after that person has been executed. *T. Sanh.* adds that both false witnesses should be convicted and punished together. Then follows a story that tells how once R. Judah ben Tabbai executed a false witness as an example "in order to root out the thinking of the Boethusians, for they usually said [that false witnesses are executed only] after the defendant has been executed."

Judah's action would be in order, according to the opinion of the narrator, only if he had brought both false witnesses to justice simultaneously. The designation of the Boethusians, of course, does not fit in the presumed historical situation approximately a half century before Herod. And it gives evidence of the Tosepta's tendency to replace the Sadducees of the Mishnah with the Boethusians.[57] Historically speaking, the text is not usable.

Thus we may summarize. The Tosepta, in contrast to the Mishnah, includes only one explicit reference to the Pharisees (*m. ®ag.* 3.35). Thus they remain completely in the background. *M. ʿErub.* 6.2 is the only Mishnah reference to the Sadducees that is without counterpart in the Tosepta. The Tosepta replaces Sadducees with Boethusians twice (*t. Yad.* 2.20 versus *m. Yad.* 4.6-8 in matters of ritual purity and civil law; *t. Sanh.* 6.6 versus *m. Mak.* 1.6 in the question of false witnesses). The Tosepta includes the following new references to the Boethusians: *t. Yoma* 1.8 (the rite for Yom Kippur), *t. Sukk.* 3.16, and *t. Roš Haš.* 1.15 (the date of the Feast of Tabernacles). A new reference to the Sadducees appears in the Tosepta in the matter of the purification of the menorah (*t. ®ag.* 3.35). Adapted from the Mishnah, we find the Sadducees in *t. Para*

---

57. The parallel *y. Sanh.* 6.5.23b omits the reference to the Boethusians. *B. Mak.* 5b and *b. ®ag.* 16b replace the Boethusians with Sadducees.

3.8 (Rite of the Red Heifer) and *t. Nid.* 5.3 (menstruating women).
Thus all three occasions in which mention of the Sadducees is made
appear in questions regarding laws of ritual purity. Nevertheless,
the Tosepta does not clearly differentiate between Boethusians and
Sadducees, for example, seeing the Boethusians as a priestly wing
of the Sadducees or an otherwise related subgroup. On the contrary,
it uses both names interchangeably: the (high) priest in *t. Yoma* and
t. Sukk. is a Boethusian, in *t. Para* a Sadducee, and in *t. Nid.* not a
Sadducee.

Where the Tosepta portrays a simple *halakic* difference between
Sadducees or Boethusians and Sadducees or rabbinic scholars, the
superiority of the rabbinic position is presupposed, but without polemic. Even in the apophthegma-like text *t. ®ag.* there is no direct
devaluation of the Sadducees. It is different where the Tosepta begins to narrate: all of these stories envision the victory of rabbinic
points of view more or less drastically. And they have deadly consequences for those who depart from them. In contrast to the Mishnah
there is no fundamentally new information about the Sadducees or
the Boethusians, just the simple joy of storytelling. We find information in the Tosepta that might be usable for historical purposes—
going beyond what the Mishnah offers—in the discussion of the
difference of opinion on the right of inheritance, the discussion of
the rites for Yom Kippur, and the Feast of Tabernacles, as well as
the festival calendar. Likewise, the label *Boethusian* is assured, even
if there are problems in making a historical evaluation.

In general, the Palestinian Talmud remains close to the Tosepta.
It extends the narrative of the Day of Atonement (*Yoma*) in a legendary manner. The Babylonian Talmud, on the other hand, attempts to lend an aura of older tradition to its stories with their
presentation as a *baraita*. In reality, it treats its versions quite freely,
giving free rein to its love of storytelling and even shaping in *b.
Men.* 65a-b a completely new story following the pattern in *b. B.
Bat.* 115b-116a. This means that the narrative *baraitot* of the Babylonian Talmud cannot be evaluated historically. It also means that
we must be skeptical about those texts for which we do not have
earlier parallels with which to compare. This is especially true of *b.
Qidd.* 66a, the story of the Pharisees' break with Alexander Jannaeus

and the murder of all the wise men, who are here clearly identified with the Pharisees. Otherwise the Pharisees appear very rarely in the Babylonian Talmud—far less than the Sadducees, for whom the majority of citations are to be eliminated for text-critical reasons (later replacements for *min*). The discussion of *m. ʿErub.* 6.2 in *b. ʿErub.* 68b, where it is even represented that the Sadducees (at least in certain points of halakah) are despised as heathen, shows how great a distance there was between the Talmud and the historical Sadducees.

The Talmud frequently relates a text of the *Scroll of Fasts* to the victory over the Sadducees in matters of the right of inheritance, the daily sacrifice, and the festival calendar (*b. Men.* 65a-b, *b. B. Bat.* 115b-116a). It is extremely improbable that the redactors of the Talmud still had genuine traditions about the factual reasons for these dates. It is more likely that they were skillfully combined with information from other sources. This also makes the Hebrew scholium on the Aramaic root text of the Scroll of Fasts unreliable as a source for the disagreement between the Pharisees and the Sadducees. Because we sometimes encounter the opinion that the Hebrew text was originally Tannaitic, we must remember that the text was a medieval compilation that had already made use of the Talmud, among other things.

3.5 Sadducees and Boethusians in ʾ*Abot de Rabbi Nathan*

In concluding, we shall look briefly at a text that portrays the origin of the Sadducees and the Boethusians from the rabbinic point of view, namely ʾ*Abot R. Nat.* B 10 and A 5 (Schechter 26). The starting point is a statement by Antigonos of Sokho in *m.* ʾ*Abot* 1.3:

> Antigonos of Sokho took over from Simeon the Righteous. He was accustomed to say, "Don't be like slaves who serve their masters for the sake of a reward, but be like slaves who do not serve their masters for the sake of a reward. And the fear of heaven be upon you.

ʾ*Abot R. Nat.* adds this sentence, "And you will receive a reward as if you had done it, in this and in the coming world." This addition points to the coming world, as does the addition in A, "With it, may your reward be doubled in the coming age." Both additions point to a possible misunderstanding of Antigonus's maxim. The following story deals with this.

> He had two students, Zadok and Boethus. And when they heard this word, they taught it to their pupils. And their pupils spoke the word from their master's mouth, but they did not tell his explanation. They said to them, "If they [you] had known, that the resurrection of the dead would be given to the righteous as a reward in the coming world, would they [you] have spoken in this way?" They left and separated themselves. And there came two groups from them, Sadducees and Boethusians—the Sadducees from the name of Zadok, and the Boethusians from the name of Boethus.

Version A, unlike B reproduced here, does not list Zadok and Boethus as the direct pupils of Antigonus but mentions both later. There are also other differences, including especially the following insertion by A.

> And they were accustomed to use silver and golden utensils all their days. This was not because they were arrogant—nevertherless, the Sadducees say, "It is a tradition with the Pharisees that they mortify the flesh in this world, nevertheless, in the coming world they have nothing.

In general ʾAbot R. Nat. B may be regarded as the older version, dating perhaps in the third century, while A may be much later. We may therefore regard B as an explanation for the frequent classification of the Sadducees into Sadducees and Boethusians in the Tosepta. There do not seem to be differences between the two groups, nor is the split attested in the text. Attempts to support the origin of the Sadducees in the Maccabean period come from the person of Antigonus: If we place his ancestor Simeon the Righteous around 200 B.C.E. (and not around 300 B.C.E., which according to Josephus would likewise be possible), we would come to the period around 170 B.C.E. for the name-giver of the the two groups. Nevertheless, both versions of the text count on a longer period for the chain of tradition, until we come to the statement of Antigonus about selfless service as a basis for the denial of a future reward. We are unable to utilize the text historically. Besides the cliché that Sadducees deny a reward in the afterlife there is an underlying name that requires explanation. Since the name Boethus is probably connected with a high priestly family that was appointed by Herod, we might naturally think that there was a split within priestly circles and their followers during the Herodian period: followers of the new high priest, even Boethusians, on one side and on the other Zadokites, representing the revivifying dream of the reestablishment of the dynasty of Zadok from the Davidic age. For this purpose, however, we do not need this story, which does not even mention priests. The later addition by A makes the Pharisees the diametric opposite of the Sadducees. The basis of the rather fairy-tale-like story of the silver and gold utensils (which is ascribed to revered rabbinic masters) could perhaps be Josephus's statement that the Sadducees met with approval only among the wealthy, but it could simply have come from the denial of future reward. Thus we learn primarily rabbinic clichés about the Sadducees, but nothing of real historical value.

Rabbinic texts are therefore useful only for certain *halakic* differences between the Sadducees and the Pharisees. Nevertheless, we will show how fuzzy this concept was in rabbinic texts (and perhaps also was in reality?) in the next section on the *halakic* positions of the Sadducees. Even about the Pharisees we do not learn nearly as much here as is usually believed. It is true that these texts can supplement certain earlier information, as well as illustrate and support it, but they do not help fill out the picture in a substantive way.[58]

58. The attempt of L. Finkelstein, "The Pharisaic Leadership" in W. D. Davies and L. Finkelstein, eds., *The Cambridge History of Judaism* (Cambridge, 1989), 2:245ff., to analyze the rabbinic texts for a history of the Pharisees since the period of Ezra can only be called an anachronism.

TWO

PHARISEES AND SADDUCEES: THEIR TEACHINGS

Now that we have completed an examination of the sources, it would still be a mistake if, as a next step, we tried to portray the history of the two schools of thought, for in order to do that we would have to make use of other texts that do not mention either Pharisees or Sadducees explicitly, though their contents make the necessary connections. If we would rather not expose ourselves to the charge of circular argumentation (in other words, classifying certain texts with the Pharisees or the Sadducees and then deriving from the texts their teachings and history—especially their pre-history), we must at first limit ourselves to explicit statements.

It is important to observe that the sources do not cover certain points that are essential for a reconstruction. Where Josephus emphasizes basic religious doctrine, characterizing the two schools as "philosophies" and mentioning the law only in general terms, the New Testament is more concerned with the religious law, which is also central to rabbinic texts. Most statements are found in at least two text groups, which gives us added surety.

1. TENETS OF FAITH

For Josephus, the critical difference between the Pharisees and the Sadducees is found in their posture toward the law and tradition. Looking at the sources, we can determine the main differences by examining the concrete teachings and practices that distinguish the two groups from each other.

1.1 Fate and Free Will

In three places Josephus sketches the religious doctrines over which the Pharisees and Sadducees differ.

> Of the two first-named schools, the Pharisees, who are considered the most accurate interpreters of the laws, and hold the position of the leading sect, attribute everything to Fate and to God; they hold that to act rightly or otherwise rests, indeed, for the most part with men, but that in each action Fate co-operates. Every soul, they maintain, is imperishable, but the soul of the good alone passes into another body, while the souls of the wicked suffer eternal punishment.
>
> The Sadducees, the second of the orders, do away with Fate altogether, and remove God beyond, not merely the commission, but the very sight, of evil. They maintain that man has the free choice of good or evil, and that it rests with each man's will whether he follows the one or the other. As for the persistence of the soul after death, penalties in the underworld, and rewards, they will have none of them. (*BJ* 2.162–65)

Josephus does not mention the attitude of the Essenes toward fate here. He does include it, however, in the other two summaries of the doctrines of the three schools, contrasting it with the position of the Pharisees:

> As for the Pharisees, they say that certain events are the work of Fate, but not all; as to other events, it depends upon ourselves whether they shall take place or not. The sect of Essenes, however, declares that Fate is mistress of all things, and that nothing befalls men unless it be in accordance with her decree. But the Sadducees do away with Fate, holding that there is no such thing and that human actions are not achieved in accordance with her decree, but that all things lie within our own power, so that we ourselves are responsible for our well-being, while we suffer misfortune through our own thoughtlessness. (*AJ* 13.172f.)

> [The Pharisees] postulate that everything is brought about by fate, still they do not deprive the human will of the pursuit of what is in man's power, since it was God's good pleasure that there be a fusion

and that the will of man with his virtue and vice should be admitted.
. . . The doctrine of the Essenes is wont to leave everything in the
hands of God. (*AJ* 18.13, 18)

In Hebrew there is no word that corresponds to the Greek
heimarmenē; apparently Josephus (perhaps even his model, Nicolas
of Damascus) simply translated the concept of divine foreknowledge and predestination into Greek philosophical terminology.[59] The
text outlines the possible attitudes on this question into three
schools, which makes us rather skeptical about the apodictic statements.[60] We have independent confirmation of this statement first
for the Essenes, for whom we have several references to belief in
divine predestination in the Qumran texts.[61] For the Pharisees we
usually refer to rabbinic statements like Akiba's in ʾAbot III.15,
"All is foreseen, but freedom of choice is given." Still, it must be
proven that this is an extension of Pharisaic thinking.[62] The middle
position, ascribed to the Pharisees, may have been more widespread
and not specifically associated with any single school.

Regarding the position ascribed to the Sadducees, we have a
parallel in the description of Epicurean concepts in *AJ* 10.278: regarding the fulfillment of the prophecies of Daniel, we see just how
mistaken the Epicureans are "who exclude foreknowledge [*pronoia*]
and do not believe that God directs events"; the world moves rather
on its own (*automatos*). It is especially noteworthy that Josephus
does not mention *heimarmenē* here, and in connection with the
various movements within Judaism he does not mention *pronoia*.[63]
The substantive parallel is uncontrovertible, yet the popular parallel

59. See G. F. Moore, *Schicksal*; L. Wächter, *Die unterschiedliche Haltung*; G.
Maier, *Mensch und freier Wille*.
60. See Schürer et al., *History of the Jewish People* 2:394.
61. See H. Lichtenberger, *Studien zum Menschenbild in Texten der Qumrange-
meinde* (Göttingen, 1980), esp. 184–89.
62. G. Maier, *Mensch und freier Wille*, 264ff., uses the *Psalms of Solomon* as
evidence for the Pharisaic idea, but first the Pharisaic origin of the text must be
clearly demonstrated.
63. This would be true even if both concepts were nearly identical in the *stoa*,
as L. Wächter, *Die unterschiedliche Haltung*, 100, emphasizes.

drawn between the Sadducees and the Epicureans remains historically unproven. Following G. Hölscher, R. Meyer summarizes: The
Sadducean school "did not deny the existence of God on a theoretical level, but practically speaking they were atheists."[64] This would
be correct if Josephus's description were correct. His attempt to
draw parallels with Greek schools of thought causes us to doubt his
precision in other matters, even if the statements may be true. Greater reliance on human capability and responsibility, for the Sadducees, could be based on their social position, but their emphasis on
the transcendence of God may very well also be involved here.[65]

1.2 Immortality, Resurrection, Reward and Punishment

According to Josephus, the second point of theological conflict concerns the immortality of the soul, as well as reward and punishment
after death. It is quite true that postbiblical Judaism replaced the
biblical anthropological unity with a more or less developed body-
soul dualism; nevertheless we can interpret Josephus's remarks on
this subject as an accommodation to his Greek readers. The point of
disagreement between the various contemporary schools of Judaism
was not the continuation of the soul after death, but the resurrection—as the New Testament makes clear. Acts 23:6-8 describes
how Paul could divide the high council in his own best interests:

> When Paul noticed that some were Sadducees and others were Phar-
> isees, he called out in the council, "Brothers, I am a Pharisee, a son
> of Pharisees. I am on trial concerning the hope of the resurrection of
> the dead." When he said this, a dissension began between the Phari-
> sees and the Sadducees, and the assembly was divided. (The Saddu-
> cees say that there is no resurrection, or angel, or spirit; but the
> Pharisees acknowledge all three.)

---

64. R. Meyer, *TWNT* 7. L. Wächter, *Die Unterschiedliche Haltung,* 106, speaks
correctly of "Josephus's hereticizing of the Sadducees who were hostile to him."

65. Thus A. J. Saldarini, *Pharisees,* 304: the Sadducean conception of foreknowledge mirrors "a post-exilic view of God as very transcendent and far from
the affairs of the Jewish nation." We should exercise care regarding the cliché that
we find again in M. Goodman, *The Ruling Class,* 79: "Sadducaism embodied a
smug self-congratulation about the status quo that only the rich accept."

The so-called Sadducee question (Mark 12:18-27) supports this statement concerning the resurrection: the Sadducees "say there is no resurrection" (Mark 12:18). We most often interpret this statement in connection with the relevant texts from Josephus that the Sadducees did not believe at all in a life after death.[66] Taken together with the previously described concept of fate, this would support their purely "here and now" orientation and their relation to the Epicureans. *ʾAbot R. Nat.* A 5 would also agree with this thesis: doubt about ultimate reward would have led the Sadducees, at least, to enjoyment of this present life. This motif is absent in the earlier version B.

M. Ber. 9.5 says the concluding formula of the prayer "from age to age" (*min ha-ʿolam we-ʿad ha-ʿolam*) would have replaced the earlier formulation "forever" (*min ha-ʿolam* or *ʿad ha-ʿolam*), since the *minim* degenerated and said that there was only one world (*ʿolam*). Later versions replaced the *minim* with the Sadducees,[67] but there is no rabbinic evidence outside of *ʾAbot R. Nat.* that the Sadducees doubted an afterlife or the resurrection.[68] We might well imagine that the Sadducees opposed the developed doctrine of the resurrection with the traditional biblical conception of Sheol, being rather skeptical regarding what we might assert concretely about life after death. It might also be conceivable that they advocated the "modern" notion of the immortality of the soul. Answers to these questions are closely connected with other theses that regard the Sadducees as either conservative followers of the ancient biblical

66. S. T. Lachs, "The Pharisees," suggests that the denial of spirits and angels in Acts 23 should be connected with the resurrection: the Sadducees deny the resurrection, "whether it be as an angel or as a spirit."

67. S. T. Lachs, "Why Was the 'Amen,'" uses the rabbinic texts completely uncritically for historical reconstruction. For him "Sadducee" was the original reading; the Pharisees wanted to control the inner attitudes of the Sadducees after they imposed the external form of the liturgy upon them.

68. In the Targum for Gen. 4:8, Cain denies the jurisdiction and mercy of God. Perhaps the text is anti-Sadducee; thus S. Isenberg, *An Anti-Sadducee Polemic*, which tries to date the motif in the first century. Nevertheless, see J. M. Bassler, "Cain and Abel in the Palestinian Targums," *JSJ* 17 (1987): 56–63, who sees this as a mixture of various ideas.

faith or as assimilated Hellenists. The former could integrate more information that we have about the Sadducees and so is more plausible, but it is not entirely provable. On the other hand, the latter belongs strictly in the realm of polemics.

According to Josephus (*BJ* 2.154-58), the Essenes advocated the doctrine that was so very enticing for many people, that the body is the transitory prison of the immortal soul. The soul is released from its chains by death, the souls of the righteous enjoy eternal reward on the other side of the ocean, and the souls of the evil are punished for eternity. *AJ* 18.18 also mentions briefly that the Essenes believed in the immortality of the soul. Since Josephus explicitly compares the Essenes' hope of an afterlife with Greek ideas, this suggests that he somewhat exaggerated these parallels. On the other hand, there is no clear evidence from Qumran to suggest that they believed in the resurrection, and the emphatically ascetic posture of the Qumran community allows a certain distance from earthly existence.

Josephus states that the Pharisees believed that there would be a transmigration of the soul only for the righteous. Apparently he means that the souls would again have a physical existence "on the other side," without identifying the body of the resurrected with the body of the deceased. According to this description and consistent with Daniel 12, there is no resurrection at all for the sinner. It is possible that Josephus simplified the views here for his audience. Nevertheless, we ought to resist the attempt to clarify the picture on the basis of contemporary resurrection narratives. In the first century ideas about the resurrection were diverse.[69] In addition, the popular method of ascribing the literature of the period of the Second Temple to the Pharisees or the Sadducees each according to the presence or absence of beliefs about the resurrection is highly debatable.[70] Since there were other schools of thought or at least

---

69. See G. Stemberger, *Der Leib der Auferstehung* (Rome, 1972).

70. As problematic as the criteria are, according to G. Baumbach, *Der sadduzäische Konsertvatismus*, 201, n. 1, we see in 1 Maccabees "the only written material to come directly from Sadducee circles." On the other hand, K.-D.

many different thinkers that cannot be classified, the concept of resurrection that Christianity as well as the rabbinate adopted was certainly too widespread in the Judaism of that time to allow us to regard it as the exclusive heritage of the Pharisees.[71]

2. DIFFERENCES WITH RESPECT TO THE LAW

Josephus did indeed emphasize the Pharisees' precision in legal affairs, and he would have us understand (in his narrative of the break between the Hasmoneans and the Pharisees) that the general populace had adopted the Pharisees' statutes and were unhappy to be separated from them. Nevertheless, he gives no details about how Pharisaic notions of the Law differed from the rest of Judaism. The New Testament in its polemic against the (scribes and) Pharisees appears to fill this gap. It is concerned with questions of ritual purity (the washing of hands, utensils, and so on), precise tithing, as well as strict observance of the Sabbath (Mark 2:23–3:6; 7:2-5; Matt. 15:2; 23:23-26; Luke 11:39, 42) and divorce. The same points also play a significant role in the religious law of the Mishnah. We may regard it as a portrayal or further development of the Pharisaic position. Nevertheless, it remains undecided how specifically Pharisaic the points mentioned here really were and to what degree they differ from the positions of the Sadducees and the Essenes, especially since all of these laws have a certain biblical basis.

2.1 The Sabbath

Jesus' disagreement with the Pharisees over the Sabbath is one of the fixed points of the Jesus tradition, even if later tradition (especially John) was highly systematized here. E. Lohse may be correct that the idea "that even Jesus himself, not just the Christian community, was in conflict with Jewish Sabbath regulations may belong

---

Schunck, *1. Makkabäerbuch,* JSHRZ (Gütersloh, 1980), 292, n. 23, calls the author "a Pharisaically minded man." There are many examples like these two.

71. Thus, correctly, for example, E. P. Sanders, *Paul,* 354.

among the most certain features of the Jesus tradition."[72] We cannot tell whether the substantive points of conflict in Mark 2:23–3:6 (grain harvest, healing) allow us to identify a particularly Pharisaic point of view regarding the Sabbath law. It nevertheless illustrates a general intensification of the Sabbath laws during the postbiblical period, which had not entirely penetrated the culture of the simple folk of Galilee, or which Jesus in his self-understanding simply ignored.

The postbiblical literature (for example, *Jub.* 2:25ff.; 50:6ff.) demonstrates how intensely the few references to resting on the Sabbath were interpreted at a later time. Nevertheless, this does not allow us to conclude that—apart from details—there were points of conflict between the various schools of Judaism at the time of Jesus. It is probably certain that we may not ascribe all of the details of rabbinic Sabbath law to the Pharisees or even generally for the time around 70 C.E.

We have a potential reference to the position of the Sadducees in the Mishnah, *'Erub.* 6.2:

> Rabban Gamaliel said: A Sadducee once lived with us in the same alley in Jerusalem and my father said to us, "Hasten and put out all the [needful] vessels in the alley before he brings out [his vessels] and so restricts you."

The text is concerned with uniting the dwellings bordering the gateway into a single, private area in the intended sense of Sabbath law, while an *'erub* is erected in the passageway. It is apparently presupposed that the Sadducee had another exit, and thus he was not dependent upon the exit and did not have to forgo his rights. Thus he did not prevent the establishment of the *'erub* as long as he did not annul his waiver with a contrary action. Why should he prevent the *'erub*? This narrative example illustrates the Mishnah that precedes it: "If a man lived in the same courtyard with a Gentile or with one who does not recognize the *'erub*, this restricts him

---

72. E. Lohse, "Jesu Worte über den Sabbat," in *Judentum, Urchristentum, Kirche*, FS J. Jeremias (Göttingen, 1960), 79–89, 84.

[from the use of the courtyard]" (*m. ʿErub.* 6.1). Thus we may surmise that the Sadducee either followed other regulations for the ʿerub or he did not recognize it all, regarding it as a legal fiction that contradicts the wording of the biblical Sabbath law. In any case, the text presupposes that the family of Gamaliel were not in an ʿerub community with Sadducees. From the New Testament we know that Gamaliel was a Pharisee. Since the Mishnah never says this explicitly, we are unable to make a generalization of the situation to all Pharisees and Sadducees. Nevertheless, the isolation of this text (which we might, at best, supplement with *t. Sukk.* 3.1, according to which the Boethusians did not approve a certain ritual on the Sabbath at the Feast of Tabernacles) at least suggests that the Sabbath law was not a significant point of conflict.

According to everything we know from Josephus and the Qumran texts, the Essenes were more strict than the Pharisees in their observance of the Sabbath. "They also keep away from work on the Sabbath even more than all the rest of the Jews" (*BJ* 2.147). They certainly had not established an ʿerub, even if CD 11.4f. is not clear: "not *yitʿareb* a person according to his will on the Sabbath." This was frequently seen as an error here and corrected to *yitraʿeb*—one ought not to *fast* on the Sabbath. If the verse is read in context with what follows, it seems more likely that an ʿerub was intended.[73] According to CD 10.20-23, they would probably have taken even more offense at the disciples' picking and eating grain than the Pharisees, nor would they have approved of a healing on the Sabbath except in case of mortal danger, according to CD 11.16.[74]

2.2 Laws Regarding Ritual Purity

Concerning handwashing before meals Mark 7:3-6 says:

---

73. Thus E. Lohse, *Die Texte aus Qumran* (Munich, 1964), translates: "No one may set up an ʿerub on the Sabbath according to his own pleasure." L. H. Schiffman, *The Halakhah,* 109, opposes this interpretation for linguistic reasons. He translates: "No one shall enter partnership . . . ," which is also not without problems.

74. For details see L. H. Schiffman, *The Halakhah,* 84–133.

(For the Pharisees, and all the Jews, do not eat unless they thoroughly wash their hands, thus observing the tradition of the elders; and they do not eat anything from the market unless they wash it; and there are many other traditions that they observe, the washing of cups and pots and bronze kettles.) So the Pharisees and the scribes asked him, "Why do your disciples not live according to the tradition of the elders, but eat with defiled hands?"

It may not be a justifiable generalization for Mark to go from the practice of the Pharisees to "all the Jews." Nevertheless, it is true that we have before us something more than an exclusively Pharisaic custom.[75] We know about the strictness of the Essenes from their own writings (see, for example, 1QS 6.16-21 for access to the food and drink of the community, likewise 4Q 514). The Sadducees of the rabbinic texts are also more stringent than the rabbinic *halakah*. Excavations in the upper city of Jerusalem have yielded many ritual baths from the time of the Second Temple. There were especially wealthy priestly families living in this fashionable quarter of the city. Of course, it would be rash to classify these directly with the Sadducees; nevertheless, a special concern for observance of the laws of ritual purity is evident here.[76]

We might object that priests had their own special rules regarding ritual purity for eating donations and holy things, while the conflict of Jesus with the Pharisees took place in Galilee far from the Temple and over a very ordinary kind of meal. A distinction must, of course, also be made between the requirement of a priestly bath or dipping the hands in a ritual bath and the simple pouring of

75. It has also been suggested that the discussion of the matter of ritual purity in Mark 7 might have originally been carried on with the Sadducees and then later transferred to the Pharisees. See G. Baumbach, *Das Sadduzäerverständnis,* 32; K. Müller, *Jesus,* 9f. For the subject of the ritual impurity of the hands alone, see R. P. Booth, *Jesus and the Laws of Purity: Tradition History and Legal History in Mark 7* (Sheffield, 1986), 156ff.

76. See N. Avigad, *Discovering Jerusalem* (Oxford, 1984), 139–43. Similar construction has been observed likewise in Jericho with the numerous priestly dwellings, E. Netzer, "Ancient Ritual Baths (Mikvaot) in Jericho," *The Jerusalem Cathedra* 2 (1982): 2:106–19.

water over the hands (cf. *m.* ®*ag.* 2.5: "One pours water over the hands for a profane and a [second] tithe, and for donations and holy things one dips [them] in").[77] For the former there is a biblical basis (Exod. 30:19, 21; 40:31), yet not for simple handwashing (at most Lev. 15:11), especially not in connection with an ordinary meal. We frequently see here the transference of priestly rules to the everyday world (see already *b.* ®*ul.* 106a); this again is especially characteristic of the Pharisees. It might be generally accurate that in this point the Pharisees were the driving force behind a development in Judaism of that time, which had extended its circles of influence. When we include the rabbinic texts, it is not always the Pharisees who make the laws of ritual purity more restrictive.[78] At least in some of the points the rabbinic texts portray the Sadducees or Boethusians as representing a stricter scale of purity.

In *m. Para* 3.7f. the rabbis vigorously defend their position that the priest who burns the red heifer can be a *tebul yom*, someone who has taken the bath of purification but without waiting until sundown, after which he would be ritually clean. This halfway step for the ritual did not satisfy the Sadducees. That would have been a simplification made by the rabbis which had not existed previously. They appear to require of the functioning priest (in the burning of the red heifer) this same intervening step, to which he must return again after the ritual: "Then the priest shall wash his clothes and bathe his body in water; he shall remain unclean until evening" (Num. 19:7; Lev. 22:7 demands that he wait until sundown after the

77. For this reason E. P. Sander's reference (*Jesus,* 185) to *m. Para* 11.5 is somewhat in error; according to him someone who, pursuant to the words of the scribes, must take a "ritual immersion" (*ha-taᶜun biᵓat mayim*), may eat profane food (according to R. Meir even a tithe). This is not concerned merely with unwashed hands! It is more likely that it is related to *y. Ber.* 8.212a. On the other hand, there is nothing from the New Testament about the kind of handwashing. We might suppose that this is merely a hygenic practice later interpreted ritually and thus made obligatory.

78. E. Rivkin, *A Hidden Revolution,* 88, interprets the requirement of simple handwashing as a dilution of the biblical command. One could say that, however, only if the handwashing had replaced a bath. Nevertheless, handwashing is demanded where the Bible does not require purification.

bath to eat the priestly donation). Still, the position of the Sadducees simply does not correspond to the wording of the Bible, which
in no way requires the ritual purity of the priest for this ritual. The
demand is first found in rabbinic writings, in which the rabbis make
an analogy between Yom Kippur and the red heifer. Thus, it is also
debatable what we might deduce from this text for the conduct of
the ritual during the period before 70 C.E. Even the execution of the
ritual itself is found only in rabbinic writings of the postbiblical
period.[79]

If the Sadducees, as suggested here, rejected a priest who was
only *tebul yom* for the ritual of the red heifer, there is a parallel in
Qumran. This is treated in a passage of a letter (as yet, unfortunately,
only published in an incomplete form) in 4Q 394-99, to which the
editors (E. Qimron and J. Strugnell) have given the title *Miqṣat
Maʿase Ha-Toro*. This fragmentary text (available in six overlapping copies) is, according to the editors, from a leader of the Qumran community, possibly from the Teacher of Righteousness himself, written to the leader of the opposition, perhaps Jonathan or
Simon. A published extract of the text[80] reads:

> And also regarding the purity of the [red] heifer of the sin offering,
> he who slaughters her, who burns her, who collects her ashes, who
> sprinkles the [water of] purification, all these [require] sunset (*le-
> haʿaribut ha-šemeš*) to be clean, so that one who is clean sprinkles
> that which is unclean.

Num. 19:7-10 demands that the one who burns the red heifer
wait until sunset, until he is clean, and likewise "someone who is
clean," who collects the ashes. Does the text address the required
state *before* the ritual or, following the Bible, after it?[81] In the

79. J. Bowman's attempt ("Did the Qumran Sect Burn the Red Heifer?" *RQ* 1
[1958]:73–84, from 1QS 3.4f.) to trace the performance of the rite in Qumran is
not entirely convincing; in any case 4Q 394-99 does not support this thesis either.
80. E. Qimron and J. Strugnell, "An Unpublished Halakhic Letter," 403.
81. Qimron and Strugnell, ibid., understand the text thus: "It declares that they
must wait after their immersion until sundown before performing their tasks."

second case the text would not address exactly the same problem as the Mishnah (purity *before* the ritual), yet it is clear that Qumran did not recognize the the concept of a *tebul yom*. Thus there is here a parallel to the position ascribed to the Sadducees in the Mishnah.[82]

The same Qumran text treats another area of the law of purification in agreement with the position that the rabbis ascribed to the Sadducees. In *m. Yad.* 4.7 the Sadducees complain that the Pharisees declare the *niṣoq*, the stream of pure liquid that flows into an unclean one, to be clean. A portion of the *halakic* letter that J. T. Milik already has published agrees with this:[83] "And also concerning the *muṣaqqot* we say that there is no cleanness in it, for the moisture of the *muṣaqqot* and that of the [vessel] that draws from them is, like them, one and the same moisture." The same expression occurs in the Temple Scroll 49.7f.: "And any nourishment upon which the water is poured (*yuṣaq*) is unclean, any drink is unclean."[84] Apparently, we are dealing with older terminology here,[85] but also with a stricter halakah that the Sadducees added to the Mishnah.

M. Yad. 4.6 has Johanan ben Zakkai say against the Pharisees that they declare, "The bones of an ass are clean, but the bones of the high priest Jochanan are unclean." Usually we assume in the commentary on this text that the Pharisees and the Sadducees are in agreement; thus it is not a disputed *halakah*. That human bones are unclean is already found in Num. 19:16. But apparently the details are controversial. In 11QT 50.5 the biblical "human bone" is amplified: a dead person, while *Sifre Num* §127 (Horowitz 165) includes the separated bones of a living person. As Y. Yadin emphasizes,[86]

---

82. Cf. 11QT 50.4, 9, 12, 15 and Y. Yadin, *The Temple Scroll* 1:340; J. M. Baumgarten, *The Pharisaic-Sadducean Controversies,* 157–61.

83. J. T. Milik in his edition of this copper scroll in DJD 3 (Oxford, 1962), 225.

84. Y. Yadin, *The Temple Scroll* 2:213, correctly compares these two texts with *m. Yad.* 4.7.

85. See also Baumgarten, *The Pharisaic-Sadducean Controversies,* 162f.

86. Y. Yadin, *The Temple Scroll* 1:135.

this is probably a polemic against other *halakic* interpretations, just as in 51.4 where the biblical "carcass" (Lev. 11:25, 28, 40) is expanded with "from their bones and their cadaver, skin, flesh, and claw"; all of these render unclean, in contrast to the rabbinic interpretation.[87] The people of Qumran also regarded animal bones as unclean, but human bones were unclean only when they came from a dead person. Thus Johanan ben Zakkai in *m. Yad.* 4 is actually quoted here also in a controversial point, and not just a place where both sides agree, in order thereby to justify with the Bible the position regarding the uncleaness of hands.

The statements of *m. Yad.* 4.6 that according to the interpretation of the Pharisees, the scriptures render the hands unclean,[88] are extremely difficult to evaulate historically. It is conceivable in connection with Mark 7 that the Sadducees recognized the *halakic* category of the uncleanness of the hands. We have no rabbinic evidence for the use of this category for the sacred Scripture (or just the Temple copy?). How would the Pharisees have been able to enforce that kind of interpretation before 70 C.E.? And what practical effects would the idea that the sacred Scripture would render the hands unclean have? It would probably have guaranteed problems for the priests in the use of the priestly donation, which was to be kept strictly ritually clean, and in cultic functions in general. Still, if we would see a struggle for control of the Bible behind such *halakah* measures, the burden of which fell upon the priesthood,[89] we

---

87. Y. Yadin, *The Temple Scroll* 1:338-41 which extracts *Yad.* 4.6 and *m. Ḥul.* 9.1 along with *Sifra Shemini* 10.2 (Weiss 55b). See also Baumgarten, *The Pharisaic-Sadducean Controversies,* 162f.

88. See finally M. Goodman, "Sacred Scripture and 'Defiling the Hands,'" *JTS* 41 (1990): 99–107.

89. Thus especially E. Rivkin, *The Pharisaic Revolution,* 260: "The priesthood was effectively disqualified from handling the Torah, since it brought with it annoying penalties." The authority of the Torah was thereby transferred from the priests to the Pharisees and the scribes. Rivkin's central thesis, that during the period of the Maccabees the Pharisees wrenched control of the law and its interpretation from the priests, rests on a historical use of rabbinic texts and has no genuine basis. See also the critique by S. N. Mason, "Priesthood": according to Josephus the Pharisees were regarded as genuine exegetes, yet "the priests are the real adepts at scriptural exegesis" (661).

must note that according to the testimony of Josephus there were also Pharisees among the priests. The text is more likely to be descriptive of the development of the early rabbinic system than historical events before 70 C.E.

T. Yad. 2.20 connects with statements about the Boethusians a passage about those who take a bath in the morning; consequently, they must regard their bodies as unclean and thus may not use the name of God. The intention was to connect opponents of the Pharisees like the Essenes with the *hemero* baptists (Eusebius, *H.E.* 4.22).[90] The addition was probably not included only because of the formal similarity. It is much more likely that although the redactors of the Tosepta may not have identified this group with the Boethusians, they were regarded as at least comparable in questions of ritual purity. Thus we have a certain lateral connection here between the Sadducees and the Essenes.

Finally, concerning the statements of *m. Nid.* 4.2 and the parallels, according to Pharisaic interpretation, Sadducee women who observed their own tradition were—like Samaritan women—regarded as perpetually unclean. This text does not give evidence of the Sadducees' neglect of the laws of ritual purity. The purification laws regarding menstruating women were biblical. It is quite inconceivable that a school of Judaism that had an association with priestly circles would not acknowledge such a biblical command in its doctrine (of course, we do not know about their practice). There may perhaps have been interpretations of this law that differed in details. Nevertheless, according to statements of the Tosepta and Talmud, Sadducee women also, with individual exceptions, observed the rabbinic *halakah*: there is hardly any distinction in the *halakah*.

The statement about the Sadducee women not following the rules regarding menstruation were made in the interest of the demarcation of "Israel." If this position had been observed historically, it would have been impossible to have social contacts or even inter-

---

90. G. Lisowsky and K. H. Rengsdorf, *Die Tosefta: Seder*, 6/3 (Stuttgart, 1967), 268; Y. Yadin, *The Temple Scroll* 1:333f. with reference to 1QM 14.2-3.

marriage between Sadducee and rabbinic families. To exclude from
Israel Sadducees, who observed their own set of rules would have
had unseen consequences: cultic community would have been impossible. All non-Sadducees would have had to separate themselves
like the community of Qumran, which in CD 12.2 forbade sexual
intercourse in Jerusalem altogether in order not to render the Temple
city unclean through menstruation (*be-niddatam*) (see also the blam-
ing in *Ps. Sol.* 8:10-12). The motif belongs in the realm of polemic
and separation, yet even in this sense, we are unable simply to
transfer the statement of *m. Nid.* 4.2 to the period before 70 C.E.

2.3 The Tithe

Num. 18:20ff. does not expressly mention from what the tithe is to
be paid, even though the payment of grain from the threshing floor
and from the contents of the wine cellar is mentioned (18:27). From
that evidence we might deduce that there was a limitation on grain,
oil, and wine (thus, for example, *Jub.* 13:26f., in Qumran 11QT 60.6,
nevertheless, 60.9 even mentions the tithe of wild honey!). In Luke
11:42 Jesus reproaches the Pharisees (in Matt. 23:23 the Pharisees
and the scribes) for tithing in herbs and spices but forgetting righteousness and love. Both passages, however, emphasize that "one
must practice the one, without neglecting the other." That means
that in this one point over which there was no conflict they were
agreed with respect to the biblical obligation to tithe even seemingly
inconsequential plants. It was obvious, and not simply limited to the
Pharisees, that a Jew who strove to observe biblical regulations did
this also regarding the tithe. It is interesting in this connection that
the Mishnah law on this subject does not treat the practice of the
time of the Second Temple. As A. J. Avery-Peck emphasizes, a
corpus of laws came into existence only after the Bar Kochba revolt

> to define membership in a sect devoted to tithing and cultic clean-
> ness . . . the Pharisees, later seen as the founders of the rabbinic
> movement, likewise distinguished themselves within the rest of the
> people of Israel on the basis of their observance of tithing restrictions
> and rules of purity. It appears clear that, whatever the character of

the Pharisaic table fellowship, its rules of conduct and modes of self-definition were not taken over by the authorities cited in Mishnah.[91]

2.4 The Pharisees—A *Ḥabura*?

If the Mishnah varies from the Pharisaic tradition in these points, we lose essential support for the general notion that the Pharisees were equivalent with the *ḥaberim*. There is no prerabbinic evidence for societies that assumed as their special obligation unusual strictness in tithing and in the question of cleanness. J. Jeremias called the Pharisees an "association" and linked the appropriate laws from the Mishnah about the *ḥaberim* with the period before 70 C.E.[92] Actually the regulations of *m. Demai* 2.2-3 appear to illustrate the disagreement between Jesus and the Pharisees in questions of table fellowship:

> He that undertakes to be trustworthy must give tithe from what he eats and not from what he sells and from what he buys [to sell again]; and he may not be the guest of an ʿAm ha-ʾareṣ. . . . He that undertakes to be an Associate (*ḥaber*) may not sell to an ʿAm ha-ʾareṣ [foodstuff that is] wet or dry, or buy from him [foodstuff that is] wet; and he may not be the guest of an ʿAm ha-ʾareṣ nor may receive him as a guest in his own raiment.

This passage describes a situation in which table fellowship is prevented between *ḥaber* and ʿam ha-ʾareṣ by questions of ritual purity and tithing. *M. ®ag.* 2.7 appears to describe the connection to the Pharisees. According to it the clothing of the ʿam ha-ʾareṣ are unclean for the *perušin* (see p. 41). Nevertheless, these *perušin* are

---

91. A. J. Avery-Peck, *Mishnah's Division of Agriculture,* 84. See also 105f.

92. J. Jeremias, *Jerusalem,* II B, 112ff. His total picture of the Pharisees (95ff.) uses the rabbinic material in a completely uncritical manner and still regards the Damascus document as a document of the Pharisees. Schürer et al., vol. 2, still use the rabbinic sources extensively and they state, "Here, a haver is one who observes the Torah, including the *paradosis tōn presbyterōn,* and is therefore identical with a Pharisee" (399). Against associating the Pharisees with the *ḥaberim* is E. Rivkin, *A Hidden Revolution,* 173–75.

not to be equated with the historic Pharisees,[93] the term simply designates people who have "separated" themselves from uneducated people who are not observant of the Law. If we had to equate the Pharisees and the *haberim*, the table fellowship that Luke frequently asserts between Jesus and the Pharisees would contradict the previously cited Mishnah. Nevertheless, such an identification cannot be proved, and it would render rather problematic J. Neusner's frequently made characterization of the Pharisees at the time of Jesus as small groups in table fellowship.[94] As A. J. Avery-Peck emphasizes, the definition of a *haber* as someone who tithes in all products and eats all meals in ritual purity is rabbinic, not something inherited from an earlier time.[95] Thus questions of purity and tithing lose their overriding significance in the disagreement between Jesus and the Pharisees.

2.5 Calendar

M. Menah. 10.3 describes the cutting of the firstfruits of the barley harvest directly after the end of the first day of Pesach, even if this is a Friday, which would abrogate the normal commandment not to harvest on the Sabbath. The reaper is supposed to ask the people

---

93. A. Oppenheimer, *The 'Am Ha-Aretz* (Leiden, 1977), 156, identifies the *perušin* here as everywhere else with the Pharisees. He also regards the *haburot* as a phenomenon of the period before 70 C.E., but he distinguishes them from the Pharisees: "By the nature of things, the haverim were very close to the Pharisees in that the latter were scrupulous about the same areas in which the haverim adopted restrictive practises. But whereas the Pharisees constituted a spiritual-social movement, the haverim belonged to closed associations" (118f.).

94. E. P. Sanders, *Jesus,* 188, correctly emphasizes that "the Mishnah too points towards defining the Pharisees as what Josephus says they were—lay experts in the law—not just a purity sect." Even before Neusner, R. Meyer (s.v. "pharisaios," *TWNT* 9:19) calls the Pharisees "only relatively small . . . associations" and connects a large number of rabbinic texts with the specifically Pharisaic *haburah*.

95. A. J. Avery-Peck, *Mishnah's Division of Agriculture,* 84. A. Büchler's study *Der Galiläische 'Am Ha'ares des zweiten Jahrhunderts* (Vienna, 1906; reprint, Hildesheim, 1968), 211f., which in many respects is now out of date, agrees with this. Also, not all organizations called *haburim* in rabbinic texts are concerned with purity and tithing but could have been charitable or burial societies; see P. H. Peli, "The Havurot that were in Jerusalem," *HUCA* 66 (1984):55–74.

whether the sun had set and whether he ought to harvest with this sickle and this basket (on the Sabbath: "on this Sabbath?"), to which the people reply three times, "Yes." Before the actual harvest is described, the text inserts a gloss:

> Wherefore was all of this? Because of the Boethusians who used to say: The *Omer* may not be reaped at the close of a festival day.

This was in regard to the exposition of Lev. 23:11, 15 *mi-moḥarat ha-šabbat*; the LXX already understood this as the day after the festival, as did the rabbis. If the Boethusians were thinking of the Sabbath in the week of Pesach, their argument would not hold in the situation when the fifteenth of Nisan was a Sabbath. With the offering of the sheaf of grain, the actual omer counting of the fifty days to the Festival of Weeks began. Its date was directly connected with the offering of the omer. *B. Menaḥ.* 65a adds the quote from the *Scroll of Fasts*, according to which the Festival of Weeks was (re)instituted.

In this question also, the position ascribed to the Boethusians (or at least a very similar interpretation) is found in Qumran. The calendar portion of the *halakah* letter from 4Q has not yet been published—thus far it does not correspond with the text reproduced in partial translation by J. T. Milik as 4Q Mishmarot.[96] In any case, the festival was established there on Sunday (the fifteenth of the third month), which corresponds to the calendar of the book of *Jubilees*. Nevertheless, we have the clear testimony of the Temple Scroll 18:11-13: the sheaf is offered on Sunday, the 26th of Nisan, and exactly seven weeks later—thus also on a Sunday—comes the Festival of Weeks. This fits perfectly with the statement of *m. Menaḥ.* 10.3 about the Boethusians.[97] The story of the Tosepta *Roš Haššana* about the witnesses bribed about the incorrect terminus of the new moon (this problem also appears already in *Jub.* 1.14, 6.34). The

96. J. T. Milik, *Volume du Congrès*, VTSUP 4 (Strasbourg, 1956; Leiden, 1957), 25.
97. See J. M. Baumgarten, *Halakhic Polemics*, 395ff., who would also understand the very fragmentary 4Q 513 in this context.

witness comes over the Path of Blood (that is, the way from Jericho). This would also fit here in Jericho, because in the first century many priests lived there,[98] as well as in Qumran.

Practical observance of different calendars in the Temple, along with multiple observance of festivals, is barely conceivable, nor is there evidence for it. We could hardly imagine that the priests would have allowed themselves to be overruled by other groups in these questions that were central to them. Thus we must imagine that there were differences of opinion among the priests themselves. The subordinated group in Qumran, with its calendar, could express its opinion about an incorrect date in the calendar only by remaining distant from the cultic activity. It is likewise conceivable that other groups of priests did not follow this course, but they were in sympathy with the Qumran calendar and did support the Qumran interpretation. The polemic of the rabbinic text is directed at them or even directly at the people of Qumran.

In the calendar of festivals, as well as the previously cited examples from the laws of purity, the rabbinic texts ascribe *halakah* concepts that are also found in Qumran to the Sadducees or the Boethusians. This prompts us to question whether when the rabbinic texts use the word *Sadducee* they mean the same groups that we know from the New Testament or Josephus. Do the rabbinic texts give no real information about the historical Sadducees? It would naturally be conceivable that there are substantive parallels between Qumran and the Sadducees (presuming that we may be permitted to regard the Sadducees as a primarily priestly determined group). This would connect with Y. Yadin's idea that the overlaps between the two groups of texts came from the fact that "*tsadoqim* in the Mishnaic usage would either be a generic term for all sorts of heretics—including the Dead Sea group—or because the latter called themselves *bne Tsadoq*."[99] We will return to this question at a later time.

---

98. J. Schwartz, "On Priests and Jericho in the Second Temple Period," *JQR* 79 (1988f.): 23–48.

99. Y. Yadin, *Biblical Archeology Today,* 430. L. H. Schiffman (ibid., 431) correctly emphasizes that the names *Sadducees, Zadokites, Boethusians,* and *Phar-*

2.6 Criminal Law

Josephus wrote that the Pharisees were generally mild in the punishment of criminals, while the Sadducees on the other hand were quite severe (*AJ* 13.294; 20.199). This is frequently combined with the *Scroll of Fasts* 12, which says that on the fourth of Tammuz the Book of Decrees was abolished. The medieval Hebrew commentary associated this with a Sadducee or Boethusian book of laws, whose decrees scholars were unable to support from the Bible, and for that reason it was abolished. We recognize this cliché already in the Babylonian Talmud. There is no real source material for the Sadducees' criminal law. Interestingly, in one case the Mishnah (*Mak.* 1.6) ascribes a milder position than that of the rabbis:

> False witnesses are put to death only after judgement has been given. For lo, the Sadducees used to say: Not until he [that was falsely accused] has been put to death, as it is written, *Life for life* (Lev. 24:18; cf. Deut. 19:21). The Sages answered: Is it not also written, *Then shall ye do unto him as he had thought to do unto his brother?* (Deut. 19:19)—thus his brother must be still alive. If so, why was it written, *Life for life*? Could it be that they were put to death so soon as their evidence was received [and found false]?—but Scripture says, *Life for life*; thus they are not put to death until judgement [of death] has been given [against him that was falsely accused].

For the Sadducees the central force of the Bible passages lies in Deut. 19:21 (*nepeš benepeš*), while the wise men (not Pharisees!) proceed from *zamam* and regard as essential the intention that initially reaches its goal with the judgment (so also in the story of Susanna in the Greek Daniel 13). The historical value of the text is debatable. Before 70 C.E. there was no Jewish court that could carry out an execution. The entire text also follows a very strict rabbinic way of thinking in which Sadducees are portrayed as opponents who are easy to best. We ought not to draw to much from this passage.

---

isees did not indicate strictly defined groups, and Qumran literature has shown us that there was a great multiplicity of groups.

Also unusable as history is the narrative of the burning at the stake of the indecent daughter of a priest (Lev. 21:9), instead of following the rabbinic interpretation that a burning wick should be put down her throat (so that her body is not burned, perhaps out of very materialistic conceptions of the resurrection, *m. Sanh.* 7.2). Rab Joseph comments in *b. Sanh.* 52b that this was determined by a court of the Sadducees. Unfortunately we have no other concrete information about a different point of view regarding Sadducean criminal law.

Thus we can summarize that the Sadducees' deviations in religious law from the practice of the Pharisees are insufficiently documented. Where there is prerabbinic evidence, as in the laws regarding ritual purity, and the festival calendar, it is difficult to distinguish between the Sadducees and the Essenes. In civil law the alleged positions of the Sadducees or the Boethusians in the questions of compensation and the right of a daughter to be an heir are not improbable, but they cannot be examined more closely. Where rabbis simply contrast their own *halakic* positions with those of the Sadducees or Boethusians, we never know to what degree this is simply an outline of *halakic* possibilities in relation to a proverbial opponent.

3. TRADITION AND
INTERPRETATION OF SCRIPTURE

3.1 The Pharisees' Strict Observance of Tradition

In the *Jewish Wars* Josephus knew that he should not say much about the attitude of the Pharisees and Sadducees toward tradition. In the *Antiquities* Josephus saw an important point in the difference between the two groups in the break between Hyrcanus and the Pharisees.

> For the present I wish merely to explain that the Pharisees had passed on to the people certain regulations handed down by former generations and not recorded in the Laws of Moses, for which reason they are rejected by the Sadducaean group, who hold that only those regulations should be considered valid which were written

down (in Scripture), and that those which had been handed down by former generations need not be observed. And concerning these matters the two parties came to have controversies and serious differences, the Sadducees having the confidence of the wealthy alone but no following among the populace, while the Pharisees have the support of the masses. (*AJ* 13.297f.)

According to *AJ* 18.408f. Salome Alexandra reintroduced the statutes that her father-in-law had abolished, "which the Pharisees had introduced in accord with the tradition of their fathers." For this reason, however, the New Testament laws of purity, as we have seen, are examples of this tradition, whose observance the Pharisees especially supported.

The tradition of the elders that is emphasized so much here has its next appearance in the Pharisees' tradition of the fathers in *AJ* 13.297 (similar to 13.408 *kata tēn patroian paradosin*—the "ancestral" tradition), or more precisely in 10.51 "the tradition of the elders" that King Josiah followed, which Josephus here would perhaps like to designate as a forerunner of the Pharisees.[100] Paul, who according to his own acknowledgement in Phil. 3:5 was originally a Pharisee, also designates himself a zealot "for the traditions of my ancestors" (Gal. 1:14) in the period before his conversion.

It is remarkable how strongly Mark emphasizes the theme of the *paradosis,* which the parallel passages either ignore entirely (Luke 11:37ff.) or greatly dilute (Matt. 15:1ff.). In Mark 7:1-13 *paradosis* is the leitmotif, first positively from the viewpoint of the Pharisees—twice—(7:3, 5): "the tradition of the elders," amplified in 7:4 with "many other traditions that they observe" (*ha parelabon*). This is interrupted with the quote from Isa. 29:13. Then follows the Christian appraisal of "human tradition" (7:8) or "your tradition" (7:9, 13) placed in the lips of Jesus. These "traditions" are contrasted with the "command" or "word of God" (7:8, 9, 13). Matt. 15:1-9, however, contrasts the "tradition of the elders" (15:2) twice with "your traditions" (15:3, 6), without devaluing "human tradition." The substantive parallel, Matthew 23, does not mention *paradosis*

100. Thus A. I. Baumgarten, *The Pharisaic Paradosis,* 65.

at all. This shift within the Synoptic tradition awakes the suspicion that within the Christian rejection of *paradosis* there is room for a positive attitude toward tradition ("human tradition" in the New Testament is otherwise mentioned only in Col. 2:8; *paradosis* is regarded as positive in 1 Cor. 11:2 and 1 Thess. 2:15; 3:6).

Whether the regulations regarding purity and tithing that are so emphasized in the New Testament were central to the *paradosis* of the Pharisees or not, we do not know. Nevertheless, it is clear from the places where Josephus and the New Testament overlap that *paradosis* was an important feature of the Pharisees. To have traditions in addition to the Torah in postbiblical Judaism cannot be regarded as characteristic of any one single group, but it is taken for granted for all. In practice an individual simply cannot live in accord with the Bible without additional traditions. How can we distinguish the *paradosis* of the Pharisees from, for example, the position of the Sadducees[101] or Essenes? If it is not simply a difference in details that makes the distinction between the various Jewish schools, we ought especially to consider two questions: How was tradition developed? And how was tradition maintained?

3.2 Differences in Scriptural Interpretation?

According to Josephus (*BJ* 1.110) the Pharisees were reputed *tous nomous akribesteron aphēgeisthai*, "to explain or interpret the law more precisely" (similar to 2.162, they are the most exacting interpreters of the law; here the verb is *exēgeisthai*).[102] *AJ* 17.41 states that they were proud *ep'exakribōsei . . . tou patriou kai nomōn hois chairei to theion*. It is more likely here also that what is being

---

101. Ibid., 64, n. 4, correctly emphasizes: "The Sadducees also observed regulations that went beyond what was written in the Pentateuch. We do not know how to reconcile these practices with their rejection of Pharisaic *paradosis*."

102. O. Michel and O. Bauernfeind, *Flavius Josephus: De Bello Judaico: Der Jüdische Krieg,* vol. 1, 2nd ed. (Munich, 1962), translates *BJ* 1.110: "a group of Jews, who have the reputation of being more pious than the others and observe the law more conscientiously." On the other hand, in 2.162, "The Pharisees are reputed to be more conscientious in scriptural interpretation." By contrast Thackery in the *Loeb Classical Library* understands—more correctly in my opinion—both passages as regarding the interpretation of the law.

emphasized is exact knowledge rather than strict observance of the traditions and laws that are pleasing to God.[103] We read the same thing in *Vita* 191: "The Pharisees have the reputation of being different from the others in their precise knowledge of the laws from the fathers" (*peri ta patria nomina dokousin tōn allōn akribeia diapherein*).[104] Especially A. I. Baumgarten has developed the idea that *akribeia* appears to have been an essential point in the promotion of the Pharisees for their group.[105] It is not just Josephus who uses the term frequently to designate the Pharisees (even where he relies upon Nikolas of Damascus), but in Acts 22:3 Paul also says of himself that he was trained at the feet of Gamaliel *kata akribeian tou patrōou nomou*, and he likewise calls the Pharisees *tēn akribestatēn hairesin* (26:5). The word family *akrib-*, which occurs seven times in Acts, is always used with concepts of learning, experience, and knowledge. For this reason we probably ought not to think of the "strictest" branch of Judaism (*NRSV* in 26:5), but rather the "most exact," probably in relation to the exposition and transmission of tradition and the Law. Interpretation rather than practice is what is being emphasized here. This is also covered by Josephus's wording, but it only fits with the polemic in Matt. 23:2-3 against the scribes and the Pharisees who sit upon the seat of Moses inflicting heavy burdens, without bearing them themselves. But in all of the polemic against them, it states that the Christians ought to do everything they say.

103. R. Marcus translates in the Loeb edition rather imprecisely: "a group of Jews priding itself on its *adherence* to ancestral custom and claiming to observe the laws of which the Deity approves."

104. L. H. Feldman in the Loeb edition: "who have the reputation of being unrivalled experts in their country's laws."

105. A. I. Baumgarten, "The Name," 416, defines the term: "*Akribeia* refers to the scrupulous exactness, accuracy in detail, and specificity of Pharisaic teaching." He attempts to connect *akribeia* with the verb *paraš*, "to connect," which in the *Qal* means "to specify." Thus, he would characterize the Pharisees as *parošim*, "those who specify" (420). Therefore, the name *Pharisee* would be a self-designation for the group. Of course, some things are still unsure here; nevertheless, it seems to me that the primary association of *akribeia* with doctrine and interpretation is essential.

This suggests that the Pharisees get their tradition especially from biblical interpretation—which in academic circles has been a controversial postion with respect to the prehistory of the Mishnah. Thus their connection with the scribes must have been especially close, but short of automatically classifying all scribes with the Pharisees, for other groups obviously had their scribes, from whom the Pharisees differed in their self-proclaimed *akribeia* (CD 6.14ff. claims this for its own group).

In the meantime, we have a clear idea of the scriptural interpretation of the Essenes from the texts of Qumran. Their peculiarities lie especially in their interpretation of prophetic texts, while their exegesis hardly exceeds the expected norms in *halakic* questions.

It is usually said of the Sadducees that they practiced an especially literal interpretation of the Bible or that they even limited themselves exclusively to the Torah. Sadducees' denial of the resurrection and angels is cited as a sign of their exclusive reliance upon the Torah. But angels are mentioned in the Torah (for example, in Genesis 18), and with just a little imagination, we can also find resurrection in the Torah, as later rabbinic interpretation demonstrates. If we look for Sadducees especially in priestly circles, we would find that an exclusive recognition (not just greater emphasis) of the Torah was not compatible with Temple cultic practice, where, at very least, Psalms were also used, and on the eve of the Day of Atonement the book of Job was read.

Some people believe that there is evidence of a very literal interpretation of the Bible in rabbinic statements about *halakot* of the *ṣaddukin*. But even if these texts portray the historic Sadducees correctly, we cannot identify a greater closeness to the biblical text in them compared with the Pharisaic or rabbinic positions; the accent is simply shifted to a different place. We can sense a more literal attitude on the part of the Sadducees toward the Bible in the question of a daughter's right to inherit. In the discussions that we quoted regarding the execution of false witnesses, the moment on the Day of Atonement in which the high priest lights the incense, or when the barley sheaf is offered and consequently the Festival of Weeks was celebrated, both sides rendered absolute opinions according to different readings of the texts. We might substantiate the rejection of a *tebul yom* for the rite of the red heifer on the basis of a lack of Bible evidence for this category of ritual purity; nevertheless, the Sadducees share the extrabiblical presuppositions for this rite. The statement of *Sifre Num* §112 (Horowitz 121) belongs in the area of polemic: "'Because of having despised the word of the Lord'—that is a Sadducee—'and broken his commandment'—that is an Epicurean" (Num. 15:31). The appended alternative interpretation relates the first half of the verse to those who "who treat the Torah spitefully" (*ha-megalle panim ba-torah*). We might simply regard the accusation to be that the Sadducees did not adopt the rabbinic interpretation of the Bible. The Babylonian Talmud develops a stereotypical caricature of the Sadducees from this: they do not know how to interpret the Bible, and when asked for biblical evidence, they are either silent or they sputter nonsense (*b. B. Bat.* 115b-116a; *b. Menaḥ.* 65a-b; the scholium to the *Scroll of Fasts* adopts the same motif). At best they are concerned—like the Boethusians in *b. Šabb.* 108a, who were working from Exod. 13:9—with the command that *tepillim* may be made only from the leather of animals that people are permitted to eat (thus, only animals that are slaughtered in a kosher way); the opposing argument by the rabbi based on Deut. 14:21 (the accent is on "eating") can only be acknowledged with praise.

Thus, from our sources we are unable to deduce anything with certainty about the Sadducees' approach to the Bible. We cannot demonstrate either the limitation of the Sadducees' Bible to the Torah or a special style of biblical interpretation. We cannot document a neglect of biblical exegesis or inadequate skills on the part of the Sadducees in this area. The sources simply have too many gaps and are too tendentious.

3.3 Transmitting the Tradition

The form in which the Pharisee *paradosis* was transmitted is also disputed. Does *AJ* 13.297, according to which the Pharisees handed down certain prescriptions "that were not designated in the law of Moses," mean that the Pharisees did not write down,[106] or only that

---

106. Thus J. M. Baumgarten, *Studies,* 18–20.

they had regulations that were not included in the law of Moses, ignoring the form of the tradition?[107] An unequivocal decision regarding the formulation is not possible. If we proceed from the idea that there were laws, generally widespread, that exceeded the written Torah and were designed to make the Torah practicable, most probably the oral character of the form of the tradition would have been emphasized here. This would be a point of contrast with the Sadducees, as well as with the Essenes and other groups. The oral character in this interpretation would then refer only to the laws, not to other traditions. It would be remarkable, indeed, that the New Testament in no way referred to an oral form of the tradition of the Pharisaic formulations.[108]

We can employ *AJ* 13.297 against the representation of the Pharisees as opponents of every extrabiblical tradition, according to which the Sadducees say "that one must keep those laws that are written, but those from the traditions of the fathers need not be observed." Usually, "that are written in the Bible" is added, even though Josephus does not expressedly say it. E. E. Urbach finds support in a Hebrew scholium to the *Scroll of Fasts* that the Sadducees did not reject tradition in principal, they just placed value in the written character of all additional laws. In that scholium a Sadducee Book of Decrees was "written and set down" (*katub u-munach*). He connects this with the talmudic narrative of Jannai's break with the Pharisees (*b. Qidd.* 66a). On the advice to kill the Pharisees, the king asks, "And what then happens to the Torah?" He receives the answer, "See, it is rolled and set down (*kerukah u-munaḥat*) in a corner. Anyone who wants to learn it, come and learn!" Urbach regards "in a corner" as polemical and believes that

107. Thus Neusner, *Pharisees* 3:163–65.

108. Even if we interpret Josephus as speaking of an oral tradition of Pharisaic laws, we could not connect this with Philo's statements regarding *nomos agraphos* or directly with the later (amoraic) rabbinic dogma of the oral Torah. For Philo, see especially I. Heinemann, "Die Lehre vom Ungeschriebenen Gesetz im Jüdischen Schrifttum," *HUCA* 4 (1927): 149–71; for the rabbinic conception, cf. P. Schäfer, *Studien zur Geschichte und Theologie des rabbinischen Judentums* (Leiden, 1978), 153–97.

we ought to read *ketubbah* instead of *kerukah,* which finds support in very late texts. Thus the Sadducees would declare that a person need not master oral tradition, ultimately that the only important thing is the written and officially set down version of the law (not just the written Torah), which anyone who wants could study.[109] The result sounds plausible, the path by which it was reached is a combination of total trust in a very late rabbinic text with an enthusiasm for hypotheses. The method is very questionable from a scholarly point of view.

In sum, there is no clear picture by which we can distinguish the individual religious schools of Judaism in questions of *halakah* or in regard to their positions on biblical exegesis and tradition. There was probably more that the Pharisees and Sadducees had in common than about which they differed. The widespread characterization of the Sadducees as a party that was assimilated, hellenized, and oriented primarily toward realistic politics (*Realpolitik*)[110] is, moreover, not substantiated. If we may not equate the rabbinic Sadducees/Boethusians in some way with the Sadducees of the Gospels, the cliché collapses completely. Even the Essenes, with all their radicality, can be called only one part of a single, but many-faceted, Judaism.

109. E. E. Urbach, "The Derasha as a Basis of the Halakha and the Problem of the Soferim" (Hebrew), *Tarbiz* 27 (1957f.): 166–82, 180f. S. Safrai, *The Literature of the Sages* (Assen, 1987), 1:41, says likewise, regarding the *Book of the Decrees,* "The Sadducees took legal decisions only according to their own written tradition, while the Pharisaic legal tradition appeared not to have been written at all." Similar also is J. M. Baumgarten, *Studies,* 22, 26.

110. Thus, for example, K. Schubert, *Die jüdische Religionsparteien,* 48, who calls the Sadducees a "middle-class national liberal party."

THREE

PHARISEES AND SADDUCEES: THEIR HISTORY

Descriptions of Jewish religious parties usually include a discussion of their history. We have put off treating the historical problems until now, because only a clear knowledge of how tendentious our sources are and how shaky the foundation upon which the classic characterizations of the individual groups stand can keep us from an all too bold drawing of sharp lines back into a very early history. The New Testament has nothing to contribute to historical research; rabbinic sources, as independent evidence of the early days of the Pharisees and Sadducees, are likewise unusable. Thus, the only explicit witness is Josephus, and he relies in part upon Nikolaus of Damascus, taking us back to the Herodian period. We do not know much about his other sources. The temptation is great to find veiled references to the two groups in other writings, but the greatest care must be taken here.

1. BEGINNINGS IN THE MACCABEAN PERIOD

BJ 1.110-12 mentions the Pharisees for the first time under Salome Alexandra, but the Sadducees and Essenes only after Judea became a Roman province in the year 6 C.E. In *AJ* 13.171-73, in the story of the high priest Jonathan (161–143 B.C.E.), Josephus makes the remark, "Now at this time there were three schools of thought among the Jews. . . ." The three groups do not play a historical role here; apparently Josephus was just inserting a note that transcended temporal boundaries into the text where it seemed to him to fit. The text interrupts the narrative just as in the portrayal in *BJ* 2.119ff. There the reason for the establishment of the *hairesis* of the Galilean Judas, which wanted to have nothing to do with the other *haireseis*, was the opportunity to insert the description of this *hairesis*. Hereby contrast, the expression *proairesis* in 170 could have occasioned the insertion of the discussion of the *hairesis*. It is at the least uncertain whether he can refer to a source for this dating;[111] thus we have no solid material for historical reconstruction. Usually, however, no problem is seen in this, and the assumption is made that at least the Pharisees were founded in the early Maccabean period, and that the Sadducees and Essenes are possibly even older.

The *hasidim* or *(H)asideans*, who were supposed to have been the predecessors of the Pharisees (and also of the Essenes, according to most authors), played an essential role in the reconstruction. The central textual evidence is 1 Macc. 2:42. The discussion in this passage regards the means by which the uprising might gain new followers. The verse reads: "At that time the community of the Hasideans joined with them. They were brave men from Israel who were all faithful to the law." In a note the German Einheitsübersetzung (united translation) explains the *hasidim* as "a Jewish community who later (150 B.C.E.) split into the Pharisees and the Essenes." What is here represented as fact summarizes a generalized perception. Nevertheless, how do we know what is being maintained here?

The Greek text has *synagōgē Asidaiōn*. It is worth noting that the term *Asidaioi*, taken from Aramaic, corresponds to the Hebrew *hasidim*. Why was the term not translated as in Ps. 149:1: Hebrew, *qehal hasidim;* LXX, *ekklēsia hosiōn*? Apparently, 1 Maccabees regarded this as a firmly established term. Thus also, in 7:13, where the *hasidim* try to achieve peace with the new high priest and the royal emissary Alcimus, or even more remarkably, in 2 Macc. 14:6, where the redeposed high priest Alcimus swears to King Demetrius "those of the Jews who are called *Hasideans* (*hoi legomenoi tōn iudaiōn asidaioi*) and are led by Judas Maccabeus, are keeping the war alive and fomenting sedition, refusing to leave the kingdom in

---

111. This is the opinion of E. Rivkin, *A Hidden Revolution,* 134f.

peace." These three texts all have occurrences of the term *hasidean*. It is noteworthy that Josephus does not use the term in his retelling of the passages from the books of Maccabees (*AJ* 12.278, 284, 296). Did this designation fall out of fashion so quickly?[112]

Who were the people that the books of Maccabees called Hasideans? The translation of 1 Macc. 2:42, "the community of the Hasideans," causes us to think of a closed group.[113] Nevertheless, the Greek article is missing before each of the two substantives. The formulation is comparable to that in 7:12 (just before the mention of the Hasideans) *synagōgē grammateōn,* which is translated as "a group of scribes." The widely contrasting treatment of the same construction shows that people already knew more about the Hasideans from other sources. It would be more correct, in any case, to translate "a group of Hasideans."[114] Thus the question of whether the Hasideans were a closed, organized community or simply a branch of contemporary Judaism remains wide open. We can deduce nothing from the term *synagōgē.*

Can we describe the Hasideans more precisely on the basis of the books of Maccabees? The name refers to their piety; the semitic form of the name is perhaps also a conservative, anti-Hellenist usage. 1 Macc. 2:42 calls them *ischyroi dynamei,* the same phrase that is applied to the young Judas Maccabeus in 2:66; even if the basic *gibbore ḥayil* often means simply "rich, prominent people,"[115] we

112. J. Kampen, *The Hasideans,* 55, believes "that a group by this name simply was not considered important by Josephus and his contemporaries." This would probably hold true only if the Hasideans were a short-lived group; it would be surprising if they were the parent group of the Pharisees (and possibly also the Essenes), to whom Josephus devoted much more attention.

113. V. Tcherikover, *Hellenistic Civilization,* 125, deduces from the citation that at the time of Judas the Hasideans were "an already established sect," who might have been founded earlier, probably at the beginning of the second century B.C.E. M. Hengel, *Judentum,* 319, speaks likewise of the "assembly of the pious" as a "clearly delineated Jewish party."

114. See, for example, J. A. Goldstein, *1 Maccabees,* 234: "a company of Pietists."

115. Thus correctly J. Kampen, *The Hasideans,* 95–114, who does not want to exclude the military component of the term, but because of the above does not

ought to think here primarily of "brave warriors." These are people who voluntarily serve in the battle for the Torah.[116] The following verses show with what zeal they and their comrades strive to achieve their goals.

Frequently the Hasideans are associated with the preceding narrative of the people who, in their search for justice and righteousness, went with their families and their possessions into the desert and were killed without resistance by the Seleucid troops, because they refused to fight on the Sabbath (2:29-38). According to this, the Hasideans were a peaceable people, who were ready to join with the Maccabees on a project only on a short-term basis, after the latter had declared that self-defense is allowed on the Sabbath.[117] The fact that, according to 7:14, they were ready at the first opportunity to declare a truce and desert the resistance would also fit with this. In reality 2:29-41 is an insertion; 2:42, with the statement about the Hasideans who joined the group around Mattathias, goes directly back to 2:27, the call of Mattathias: "Follow me . . . everyone of you who is zealous for the law and strives to maintain the covenant." We are unable to deduce anything about the Hasideans from 2:29ff.[118]

---

want to view the term solely in a military manner. We should note that the LXX does not translate *gibbor ḥayil* in the sense "rich, prominent man" with *ischyros dynamei* but with *dynatos ischyi*—for example, in Ruth 2:1; 2 Kings 15:20; 2 Chron. 25:6. There may perhaps be a difference in meaning here. It should be mentioned that L. Finkelstein, *The Pharisees,* 573, 592, and elsewhere, calls the Hasideans, the plebeians. There is likewise as little evidence for this as for many other statements in his highly influential work.

116. *Pas ho hekousiazomenos tō nomō,* "all who volunteered in defense of the Torah" (J. A. Goldstein, *1 Maccabees,* 235).

117. Thus, for example, O. Plöger, *Theokratie,* 16.

118. Cf. P. Davies, *Hasidism,* 113f. H. Kampen, *The Hasideans,* 70ff., limits the insertion to 2:29-38, but he does not regard the people in this passage as the Hasideans. Josephus (*AJ* 12.272, 275) indeed mistakenly connected these two narratives. Nevertheless, he "does not fall into the trap which has caught many modern interpreters, i.e., that 1 Maccabees 2 is the record of a grand alliance between the religious Hasideans and the political Maccabees" (76).

Nor is 7:12f. entirely clear:

> Then a group of scribes appeared in a body before Alcimus and
> Bacchides to ask for just terms. The Hasideans were first among the
> Israelites to seek peace from them.

This consciously literal translation shows at once the dilemma of
whether the Hasideans here were simply the leading citizens of
Israel (corresponding to a potential interpretation of *ischyroi
dynamei* in 2:42), or whether they were the first people to sue for
peace. It is not clear what the relationship of the Hasideans was to
the previously mentioned scribes. Were they two groups who were
working for peace, or were they the same group?[119] We cannot
come to a clear decision; there are probably at least overlaps between the two groups. According to the text, after the establishment
of a legitimate high priest the Hasideans were no longer interested
in a continuation of the fight. Their voluntary engagement on behalf
of the Torah had apparently achieved its goal—they noticed too late
that the opposition had misused their trust. To designate them as
pacifists on the basis of this position exceeds what is in the text,
especially since 2:42 characterizes them as powerful. After they
realized that they had been deceived, they (or at least a portion of
them) may have taken up the struggle again. When Alcimus charges
them with being warlike and seditious, this must not be—apart
from exaggerations—entirely false.[120]

These few statements are all that we have that speak explicitly
about the Hasideans; they were probably a conservative branch of
Judaism during the Maccabean period. The upper class were mem-

119. Thus V. Tcherikover, *Hellenistic Civilization,* 125, "a special sect among
the scribes, the sect of the Hasidim"; cf. 197: "the Hasidim were the chief scribes
and authoritative interpreters of the regulations and commandments of the Torah."

120. P. Davies, *Hasidism,* 139f., believes that 1 Maccabees, as a piece of
Hasmonean propaganda, consciously diminishes the achievements of the
Hasideans, because they felt that the ideals for which they struggled had been
betrayed by the Hasmoneans, and they wanted to say, regarding the tension in 2
Maccabees 14, that they were at the center of the resistance against Alcimus.

bers, and they had connections with the scribes.[121] At least a portion of them fought fanatically on the side of the Maccabees, but they also retreated from battle after they achieved the portion of their goal that seemed essential.

All further historical reconstructions are fundamentally derived from 1 Macc. 2:29-38, which says nothing about the Hasideans. When the group described here refused to defend itself on the Sabbath, this is regarded as pacifism and refusal to act (in reality the text says nothing about a general attitude but speaks only of an extreme Sabbath rest). Citing Dan 2:34, 45; 8:25, where the essential elements in history are described without human contribution, O. Plöger suggests that "the rather passive, but no less faithful posture of the book of Daniel" agrees well with the description of the Hasideans in 1 Maccabees 2.[122] From there it is not a very great step to the idea that the writer of Daniel might be an exponent of the Hasidean group.[123] With the openhearted claim that "with the reconstruction of a historical or spiritual historical development we must proceed broadly and may have to overlook some things,"[124] Plöger then connects the Hasideans with apocalypticism,[125]

121. J. Kampen, *The Hasideans,* 215, 222, believes that he can make the connection from scribal elements of the Hasideans to the later Pharisees. This is, indeed, possible but cannot be proved.

122. O. Plöger, *Theokratie,* 27.

123. O. Plöger, *Theokratie,* 33. Likewise idem, *Das Buch Daniel,* KAT (Gütersloh, 1965), 30. This thesis, reaching far back, is nearly *opinio communis.* Thus, for example, also A. A. Di Lella, *The Book of Daniel,* AB (Garden City, N.Y., 1978), 43: "The Book of Daniel as a whole may rightly be viewed as a pacifistic manifesto of the Hasidism." In contrast, correctly, is J. J. Collins, *The Apocalyptic Vision of the Book of Daniel* (Missoula, Mont., 1977), 214: "Daniel differs from what we know of the Hasidim in the methods of resistance which it advocates."

124. O. Plöger, *Theokratie,* 41.

125. Detailed in connection with Plöger, is M. Hengel, *Judentum,* 319–81: "The Chasidim and the first high point in Jewish apocalyptic." Critical of this is J. C. H. Lebram, "Apokalyptik und Hellenismus im Buche Daniel," *VT* 20 (1970): 503–24, especially 522–24; G. W. E. Nickelsburg, "Social Aspects of Palestinian Apocalypticism," in *Apocalypticism in the Mediterranean World and the Near East,* ed., D. Hellholm (Tübingen, 1983), 641–54.

drawing the line back to the late prophets as well as forward to the
Pharisees and the Essenes, "both groups, that we may rightly regard
as later manifestations of the earlier Hasideans."[126]

Since 1 Macc. 2:29-38 is independent of the passage that follows
on the Hasideans, however, we may at most connect these people
(who are not further described but are not Hasideans) with the book
of Daniel. Nevertheless, the connecting points here are so modest
that we may not simply equate the spirituality of this group with
that of the group behind Daniel. In addition, the statement in Dan.
11:33f. that "the wise among the people . . . shall receive a little
help, and many shall join them insincerely" cannot be interpreted as
directly connected with a short-term alliance between the Hasideans
and the Maccabees. If we are permitted to make such a direct connection of 1 Macc. 2:39ff. with this text, it is more likely between
the Maccabees and the Hasideans and others among the "quiet"
groups behind Daniel, who can be designated as a short-term help.
That the Pharisees, like the Essenes, adopted the book of Daniel in
their sacred writings does not mean that both movements derive
from the group responsible for Daniel. As already mentioned, for
the Essenes and Qumran there is to date no attestation of belief in
the resurrection, as in Dan. 12:2. On the other hand, the wording of
11:34, that many joined "insincerely" (*ba-halaqlaqqot*, cf. 11:21,
32), causes us to think of the designation of opponents as *dorše ha-
halaqot* found frequently in Qumran and usually identified with the
Pharisees. A direct classification of Daniel (or the later branches of
Judaism) with the groups mentioned in 1 and 2 Maccabees probably
demands too much from the text.

Since the Hasidean thesis has proven unusable, are there other
ways to reconstruct an early history of the Pharisees, Sadducees,
and Essenes? R. Beckwith believes that he can make a probable
reconstruction of the history of ideas, and "that the tendencies man-
ifested as three rival parties after the hellenizing crisis of 175–152

---

126. O Plöger, *Theokratie*, 30. The line connecting Hasideans and the Essenes
allows M. Hengel, *Judentum*, 320, from CD 1.5-12, to deduce that the Hasideans
were established between 175 and 170 B.C.E.

B.C. were already present as distinct school of thought (proto-Pharisaic, proto-Sadducean, and proto-Essene) three quarters of a century earlier."[127] He lists the belief in angels, an afterlife, the date for the offering of the first harvest and Festival of Weeks, as well as the moon calendar, as earlier attested Pharisaic positions (in Sirach as well as in the LXX in the Pentateuch); for the Essenes he lists (supported by *1 Enoch* 1-36 and 72-82) calendar, predestination, doctrine of angels, eschatology, asceticism, pacifism, and others. The lack of evidence for the Sadducees ought not to be of concern, since there is no literature on them later, either.

Even the manner in which Beckwith identifies Sirach as a proto-Pharisaic writing—the belief there in angels and afterlife excludes the Sadducees, and the moon calendar excludes the Essenes—is quite problematic:[128] are we really dealing only with these three groups? How do we explain the lack of a concept of resurrection in Sirach by this line of argument? It is obvious that the positions later represented by other groups had a long prehistory, but this says nothing about those who were the predecessors of these groups. Beckwith holds that the Pharisees were the preservers of the old traditions, and the Sadducees as biblicists and also the Essenes were reform movements. If this is true, the Pharisees must have been founded earlier than the other two groups. He concludes with a very speculative reconstruction, using the late biblical texts as well as Josephus and rabbinic statements (such as that on the "Great Synod"), that "the Pharisaic movement arose not later than 340 B.C.E.[129] The books of Tobit and Judith may be evidence of early Pharisaism. We may find in them the efforts of the Pharisaic *ḥaburot* regarding

---

127. R. Beckwith, *The Pre-History,* 4f.

128. Thus, for example, G. Sauer, *Jesus Sirach,* JSHRZ (Gütersloh, 1981), 492, emphasizes other particulars in Sirach—temple cult, the greatest praise of the high priest Simon—and excludes the idea that Sirach disputes "the claim of other Jewish spiritual movements of the time, especially of Pharisaism. He may thereby be regarded as an adherent of the Sadducean party who, for this reason, rejected the Pharisee's spiritual posture." The method of classification thus proves to be highly questionable.

129. R. Beckwith, *The Pre-History,* 31.

tithing (Tob. 1:6-8; Jdt. 11:13) and purity in eating (Tob. 2:5; Jdt. 12:5-9), "since the Pharisaism reflected in them is of a primitive character, it would probably be right to regard the two works as being (along with the Septuagint Pentateuch and Ecclesiasticus) the earliest Pharisaic writings we possess."[130] Around the middle of the third century the proto-Essenes and the proto-Sadducees were added as "reforming schools of piety, under priestly scribes."[131] Still in the Maccabean period all three groups might have been lumped together under the name *hasidim*, before there was a crisis and break between them because of a variety of developments.

Beckwith's opinion, which has been given somewhat more thorough treatment here, makes it obvious how difficult it is to reconstruct a prehistory of the various schools of piety if we do not want to separate the individual sources or connect various individual bits of evidence directly to the later schools. Thus, we will not be able to appreciate either the variety in Judaism of the Persian-Hellenistic period, about which we still know so little, or the uniqueness of the respective sources.

It is as difficult to reconstruct a more precise prehistory of the three religious schools as it is to demonstrate their provenance from the Hasidean movement. We also lack criteria to support the correctness of Josephus's temporal classification (*AJ* 13.171-73) and the existence of the three groups under Jonathan Maccabeus.[132]

2. THE HASMONEAN PERIOD

In *BJ* the Pharisees do not appear before Alexandra Salome. In contrast, *AJ* supplements the earlier report with additional material,

---

130. Ibid., 30.
131. Ibid., 39.
132. The tenuous nature of the evidence is clear in R. Beckwith, *The Pre-History*, 36. For the Essenes he cites archeological evidence; for the Pharisees, the chain of tradition from *m. ʾAbot*; for the Sadducees, the tradition in *ʾAbot R. Nat.* 5. These texts are not only questionable in and of themselves, but they also give no data! Rather more plausible is L. I. Levine, *The Political Struggle,* 63–65, who makes the founding of these groups during this period more plausible on the basis of general circumstances of the period, yet in a strict sense he does not prove it.

including the narratives about the Pharisees and the Sadducees. *AJ* 13.288-96 describes the break between John Hyrcanus and the Pharisees and his transition to the side of the Sadducees. In connection with the conquest of Samaria (108 B.C.E.), 13.288 states that the successes of Hyrcanus and his sons aroused the jealousy of the Jews, and the Pharisees were especially ill disposed toward them.

Thereafter follows the narrative of the banquet that Hyrcanus gave for the Pharisees, which was full of harmony, until one single Pharisee of poor character mentioned the rumor that Hyrcanus's mother had once been a prisoner. Thus, his heritage was suspect, and he was unfit to be the high priest. Another person who was present, a Sadducee who was on the best of terms with Hyrcanus, convinced him that this was the opinion of all of the Pharisees. Hyrcanus became so angry about it that he transferred his loyalty to the Sadducees and forbade all of the rules of the Pharisees. Because of this, he made himself hated all the more by the people. The entire affair was then a tragic chain of anger, intrigue, and misunderstanding.

Josephus says nothing about the further development of the strife between Hyrcanus and the Pharisees. For more information he refers to his later description. Nevertheless, he closes in 299f. with the succinct note that Hyrcanus was able to quiet the unrest and do it with a wonderful reputation as a glorious ruler. Furthermore, there is no more mention of the strife with the Pharisees in the discussion of Hyrcanus's successor Aristobulous.

AJ 13.372 refers to a revolt among the people against Alexander Jannaeus during the Feast of Tabernacles, and in this context mentions an accusation by the people against the king that he descended from a prisoner and for that reason was unfit to be high priest. There is as little discussion of the Pharisees as in the following description of the civil war (376ff.); after achieving his victory, Jannaeus had about 800 of his opponents crucified in Jerusalem, and 8,000 more fled the country. Only on his deathbed does Jannaeus speak of the Pharisees (otherwise unmentioned during his reign). Before he died, he advised Salome Alexandra, after her return to Jerusalem, to cede certain powers to the Pharisees, who had much influence among the people, and she did it.

> ... and she permitted the Pharisees to do as they liked in all matters, and also commanded the people to obey them; and whatever regulations, introduced by the Pharisees in accordance with the tradition of their fathers, had been abolished by her father-in-law Hyrcanus, these she again restored. And so, while she had the title of sovereign, the Pharisees had the power. (*AJ* 13.408f.)

The sequence of events described here concerning the break between Hycanus and the Pharisees and the preference for the Sadducees over the civil war under Alexander Jannaeus, up to the reestablishment of the Pharisees under Salome Alexandra, is usually regarded as historically reliable,[133] but it is not without difficulties. It is striking how inconsequential Hyrcanus's quarrel with the Pharisees was: he was able to suppress unrest without a problem and rule happily until his death. In contrast, Jannaeus always had the greatest domestic political difficulties; nevertheless, at his death he remembered that all his troubles went back to the Pharisees and advised his wife to let them come to power again. The smallest charge we are compelled to level against Josephus as a historian is that his narrative is full of holes and very disjointed.

It is quite instructive to make a comparison with the parallel passage in *BJ*. Without naming the Pharisees and Sadducees, *BJ* 1.67 speaks of a revolt among the envious in the population, which Hyrcanus managed to quell without difficulty. *AJ* divides this observation in two (13.288, 299) by means of the insertion of the fateful banquet that Hyrcanus gave for the Pharisees. The transition was not made in a particularly skillful manner: Josephus amplifies the statement taken from *BJ* about the envy of the people with an observation that the Pharisees were very hostile toward Hyrcanus. Nevertheless, the narrative that follows immediately calls Hyrcanus

---

133. Thus, for example, Schürer, *History of the Jewish People,* 1:211, and finally A. J. Saldarini, *Pharisees,* 86f., who sees the Pharisees as Hyrcanus's clients: "This political patron-client relationship explains why Hyrcanus held a banquet for his valuable and influential clients and why the Pharisees tactfully praised their powerful patron" (87). What is sociologically plausible is not necessarily historically useful.

a favorite pupil of the Pharisees. After the consequent break and the nullification of the Pharisees' regulations, we read that for those reasons the general populace hated him and his sons (296), even though at the outset (288) he was talking about the envy of the people. Josephus never fulfilled his promise to give details later. He only made a few remarks here about the Pharisees and Sadducees and then continued onward from where he had interrupted his account from *BJ*, stating that Hyrcanus suppressed the rebellion (*stasis*), but the narrative never mentioned it before.[134]

Thus, it is certain that Josephus mechanically inserted a narrative here (amplified with his own observations regarding the religious parties). There is a very similar narrative in the Talmud (*b. Qidd.* 66a) about King Jannaeus.[135] Did Josephus incorrectly place an unattached (travel?) narrative?[136] The fact that the entire episode has no continuation in the broader narrative would speak in favor of this idea.[137] On the other hand, the dying Jannaeus traced all of his

134. R. Marcus comments in the Loeb edition on this passage (13.299, n. *f*): "Meaning the opposition of the Pharisees to Hyrcanus and his sons, as is more clearly stated in his parallel in B.J." However, there is nothing there that is not also adopted by *AJ*; the Pharisees, on the other hand, are not mentioned there at all! His attempt to integrate the story into this context is also apparent in Marcus's translation of 296: "*grew* the hatred of the masses" for *misos . . . egeneto.*

135. Already I. Halevy, "Les sources talmudiques de l'histoire juive," *REJ* 35 (1897): 213–23, addressed his attention to the stylistic characteristics of the text and concluded that there was a written source. J. Neusner, *The Rabbinic Traditions,* 1:176, proposes a common source for Josephus and the Talmud. Idem, *Josephus' Pharisees,* 285f.: "Either Josephus copied from a Hebrew source, or the talmudic narrator copied from Josephus, or both relied on a third authority."

136. See, for example, G. Alon, *The Attitude,* 26, according to which *Qidd.* 66a is to be preferred over Josephus, and there might never have been a conflict between Hyrcanus and the Pharisees. Likewise, J. A. Goldstein, *I Maccabees,* 66ff., and M. J. Geller, *Alexander Jannaeus,* 210f.: because of the references to Modiin in his source, Josephus replaced Yannai with Hyrcanus.

137. This break also remains without continuation in the rabbinic tradition, which describes John Hyrcanus generally as a good high priest (see P. Kieval, *The Talmudic View,* 39ff.), even if a *baraita* knows of his change to the Sadducees: "Jochanan the high priest served eighty years as high priest, yet in the end he became a Sadducee" (*Ber.* 29a). G. Alon, *The Attitude,* 26, n. 22, regards this text as late and dependent upon *m. ʾAbot* 2.4.

problems to the Pharisees, even though Josephus's description never mentions them during his reign.[138]

It is, however, noteworthy that the accusation that at least one person makes against the king in the narrative of Hyrcanus and the Pharisees—that his mother may have been a prisoner of war and that he as a consequence could not be high priest—reappears in *AJ* 13.372 against Alexander Jannaeus. Here also Josephus amplifies the account in *BJ* 1.88, which states only that there was an uprising among the Jewish people during a feast, and that the king was able to put down the rebellion with his mercenaries. *AJ* 13.372f. adds to this that it was the Feast of Tabernacles and that the king was ready to sacrifice at the altar when the people threw the citrons at him that they had for the festival. He was insulted by the people because he was descended from a prisoner. Naturally, it is conceivable that the accusation of illegitimacy for a high priest within the dynasty returned frequently and played a part here as well as there. It appeared both times after successful campaigns of the ruler; the military activities of a prince apparently made him unfit, at least in some circles, for the office of high priest (according to 1 Chron. 28:3 even David was not permitted to build the Temple because his hands had spilled blood); this, however, limits the charge to the possibility that the wife of a king who was engaged in war could fall into the hands of the enemy. Curiously, heritage played no role otherwise; Hasmoneans were not rejected because they did not descend from the family of Zadok. This is not a matter of the separation of the royalty and the priesthood. There was no dispute over whether the Hasmoneans might claim the royal title, even though they were not descended from the family of David—not even from the house of Judah. The resistance to the Hasmonean priesthood fits naturally in the scene with Alexander Jannaeus, who is about to sacrifice. It fits especially well, and even better than in the story of

138. L. I. Levine, *The Political Struggle,* 69, attempts to explain Josephus's silence as intentional: he would not have wanted to describe the Pharisees to a Roman readership as seditious, and a danger to the national order. It has already been demonstrated that such intentions are not attested in Josephus.

Hyrcanus's banquet. Perhaps we may regard this as an indication that this story was originally connected with Jannaeus.

It is also worthy of note that the story of the high priest before the altar at whom the people threw citrons at the Feast of Tabernacles also has a rabbinic parallel (*m. Sukk.* 4.9), even if it may not be connected with the same fundamental story. In the Mishnah the high priest is not accused because of his parentage, but because of the conducting of the ritual.[139] It should also be mentioned that the Talmud states frequently that Jannaeus killed nearly all the rabbis (thus *b. Qidd.* 66a, *b. Ber.* 48a, and elsewhere).[140] Apparently, the Josephus tradition of the 800 is involved here in ways that we are unable to ascertain more closely. These episodes (and Jannaeus's cruelty in general) are also mirrored in the Nahum pesher of Qumran (see below) and may have been generally kept alive in folk tales. Finally, *b. Sota* 22b also knows that, Jannaeus urged his wife not to be afraid of the Pharisees, but only of those people who behave dishonorably. This is a warning that, in view of the friendly relations between Alexandra and the wise men in the rabbinic tradition, is unnecessary and probably is an echo of the Josephus tradition. This accumulation of parallels between the Babylonian Talmud and Josephus is striking. The paths from the parallel material to Josephus in the rabbinic literature are not easy to determine,[141] but we may conclude with some certainty that there was direct dependence by the rabbis upon Josephus. It is clear, however, that in these cases both rely on anecdotal folk tales, whose arrangement in an incorrect sequence in a larger narrative context is a constant problem.

Thus, the story of the break between Hyrcanus and the Pharisees is historically dubious: it would be more plausible to date it during

139. Thus correctly J. Efron, *Studies,* 169.

140. The rabbinic tradition of Palestine still does not know this motif. J. Efron, *Studies,* 143–218, presents an outstanding analysis of the rabbinic texts on John Hyrcanus, Alexander Jannaeus, and Salome Alexandra in comparison with Josephus. Yet I do not believe that *Qidd.* 66a intentionally replaced Hyrcanus, who was admired by the rabbis, with Jannaeus (177).

141. For the problem, see S. J. D. Cohen, "Parallel Historical Tradition in Josephus and Rabbinic Literature," *Proceeding of the Ninth World Congress of Jewish Studies*, B/I (Jerusalem, 1986), 7–14.

the time of Alexander Jannaeus for a variety of reasons.[142] Probably, we could hardly trace the Pharisees as an organized group
before Jannaeus by using historical methods, even if the spiritual
groups that precede the Pharisees are, of course, much older. The
same is true of the Sadducees, whom—with the exception of a
plotter in the banquet story—Josephus does not mention as playing
a part until the last decades of the Second Temple.

After a nearly complete exposition the Nahum pesher of Qumran
describes the events under Jannaeus and the following decades.
Thus, it is a valuable supplement to Josephus's description.[143] 4Qp-
Nah 3-4 1.2 interprets Nahum 2:12b, "[Deme]trius, king of Greece,
who on the advice of those who teach plainly (*dorše ha-ḥalaqot*),
sought to come to Jerusalem," which God, however, did not permit.
This coincides with 13.376, according to which the people sought
help from Demetrius (III Eukairos) against Alexander Jannaeus.
The pesher refers to him as a "lion of wrath" (once also in 4QpHos[b]
2.2, but out of context). The *dorše ha-ḥalaqot* usually are the Pharisees,[144] but could also be generally representative of a non-Qumran
biblical interpretation and *halakah*. Line seven mentions them again,
but a lacuna in the text before it renders the interpretation uncertain.
Apparently the text was speaking about the vengeance of the lions
of wrath toward "those who teach plainly. And he hanged living
people [on the tree]." This quite probably refers to Jannaeus's cruci-
fixion of 800 of his opponents. We are unable to tell for certain
whether the pesher regarded the victims as Pharisees (which Josephus does not expressly say) because of the unclarity of the text.

We are on surer ground, in any case, from Salome Alexandra on.
Josephus emphasizes the dominant position of the Pharisees during

---

142. L. I. Levine, *The Political Struggle,* 70ff., offers a good analysis of the
story of the break between Hyrcanus and the Pharisees. He sees its dubious nature
clearly. Nevertheless, he suggests that in it we can see the Pharisaic version of the
actual break, which in reality may be based in the increasing military activity of
the Hasmoneans and the increasing independence of the military leadership, whose
membership certainly included priests.

143. Thus, especially D. Flusser, *Pharisees.* Additional literature and a short
summary in M. P. Horgan, *Pesharim,* 158–62.

her time both in *AJ* and *BJ*. Now the Pharisees are also a political power. *BJ* 1.110-12 speaks of the ever increasing influence of the Pharisees upon Salome, who was herself an active ruler, maintaining control of government and the military force. *AJ* 13.401f. traces the influence of the Pharisees back to Alexander Jannaeus's final directive—that Salome should cede royal power to the Pharisees. Ultimately, she possessed only the title, while the Pharisees exercised the real power, functioning like despots (409).

4QpNah 3-4 2.4-10 speaks of the "rule of those who teach plainly," of many dead people and exiles out of fear of the enemy; "honored ones and rulers will fall on account of what they have to say." This fits most appropriately with Josephus's statements about the period of Alexandra: the Pharisees had Diogenes executed because he advised Jannaeus in the decision to crucify the 800 (*BJ* 1.113, *AJ* 13.410), and they also persecute others whom they regarded as responsible. A number of significant people fled to Aristobulus, and his mother spared their lives on the condition that they disperse themselves throughout the country (*BJ* 1.114f.). According to *AJ* 13.414ff. they suggested to Alexandra that Aretas the Arab and other princes would take them on as mercenaries and dispatch them for protection into different garrisons. Only now are the persecuted Pharisees characterized as soldiers. L. I. Levine[145] would see Sadducees not named by Josephus under Alexander Jannaeus and Salome Alexandra. He uses the Pesher Nahum for support. This Pesher Nahum speaks of the downfall of the council of those who teach plainly, continuing:

"Are you better than Amon which lay among the rivers?" (Nah 3:8a)?
Interpreted, *Amon* is Manasseh; and the *rivers* are the great men of Manasseh, the honorable men of Manasseh.
"Which was surrounded by waters, whose rampart was the sea and whose walls were waters" (Nah 3:8b).
Interpreted, These are her valiant men, her almighty warriors.

144. This is thoroughly established by J. Maier, "Weitere Stücke," 233–44.
145. L. I. Levine, *The Political Struggle,* 67f.

"Ethiopia [and Egypt] were her [limitless] strength" (Nah 3:9a)
[Interpreted] . . .
["Put and the Libyans were your helpers"] (Nah 3:9b).
Interpreted, these are the wicked of [Judah], the House of Separation, who joined Manasseh.
"Yet she was exiled; she went into captivity. Her children were crushed at the top of all the streets. They cast lots for her honorable men, and all her great men were bound with chains" (Nah 3:10).
Interpreted, this concerns Manasseh in the final age, whose kingdom shall be brought low by [Israel . . .] his wives, his children, and his little ones shall go into captivity. His mighty men and honorable [shall perish] by the sword.
"[You shall be drunk] and be stupified (Nah 3:11).
Interpreted, this concerns the wicked of E[phraim . . .] whose cup shall come after Manasseh . . . (4QpNah 3-4 3.8-4.6).

Usually Manasseh is interpreted as being "the Sadducees," an interpretation at which Flusser and others have arrived by a kind of process of elimination. Since the *dorše ha-ḥalaqot* are the Pharisees and thus are (or their membership is) comparable with Ephraim, only the Sadducees are left to be Manasseh.[146] That was a much too rapid trip through the probably far more complex reality of Judaism in the period of the Second Temple. The text is not so clear that we can connect names and particular groups with certainty. However, much more problematic is the equating of Manasseh in this text

---

146. D. Flusser, *Pharisäer,* 134ff. Flusser's deduction from his interpretation of Manasseh in the Qumran texts is even more problematic: the Sadducees were probably "not a religious community in the true sense of the word, like the Pharisees and the Essenes, but more a political party than a religious community" (154). D. Pardee, "A Restudy of the Commentary on Psalm 37 from Qumran Cave 4," *RQ* 8 (1972–75): 163–94, 179f., warns against such a mechanical interpretation of Ephraim and Manasseh, who are the opponents of the priests in 4QpPs^a 2.18-20. The pair—Ephraim and Manasseh—might simply designate any group in opposition. See also M. P. Horgan, *Pesharim,* 194, who accepts the interpetation as the Pharisees and the Sadducees, nevertheless, she sees "no clear allusions to indentifiable historical events" in 4QpPs^a. On the other hand, L. I. Levine, *The Political Struggle,* 80, sees a reference to the time of Simeon who joined the Pharisees and Sadducees together in his policies.

with the warriors, and from thence the identification of the people, who during the Pharisee leadership had to go back to the fortresses, as Sadducee warrior-priests, as Levine tries to do. We are unable to find historically reliable statements about the Sadducees for this period.

Josephus does not give us details about the Pharisees' positive accomplishments during this period; he mentions only the reintroduction of the Pharisaic traditions (*AJ* 13.408). There is a great temptation to use rabbinic sources to fill Josephus's silence with material on Simeon ben Shetah (who, according to later tradition, was reputed to be a brother of Salome Alexandra). Levine attempts to make plausible the evolution of the Sanhedrin from a Sadducee to a Pharisee institution, the participation of Pharisees in trials of a capital nature, and their influence on the educational system, marriage law, and so on at this time. In so doing, he lends much too much historical significance to these texts, even if he makes a pro forma limitation: "It is clear that not all of these traditions are historical and the *haggadah* component in them is not insignificant; nevertheless, the concentration upon traditions that ben Shetah connected with public life is evidence of his intensive activity in this area."[147]

Since *AJ* 13.411ff. demonstrates that Aristobolus II, was on the side of the nobility, who protested against the Pharisees' politics and then were permitted to withdraw into a few fortresses, the Sadducees are usually interpreted as followers of Aristobolus and the Pharisees as partisans of Hyrcanus II in the Hasmonean sibling rivalry of the following year, which ultimately led to the capture of Jerusalem by Pompey.[148] If the equation of the superior military force with the Sadducees is already questionable, that of the followers of Hyrcanus with the Pharisees is even more so. When we follow the narrative of *AJ* 14.40f., which states that in addition to the delegations of Aristobolus and Hyrcanus there was a legation

147. L. I. Levine, *The Political Struggle,* 67.

148. Against this thesis, insofar as it concerns the Pharisees, is G. Alon, *The Attitude of the Pharisees,* 27–29: Aristobolus would first have supported himself with the Sadducees, but would then have also won over the Pharisees. J. Le

from the Jewish people that came to Pompey and declared that they wanted neither of the two (*BJ* 1.131 lacks this), we may take this to mean that many people joined neither of the two parties. G. Alon opines that the people might have been represented by the Pharisees here and that we might conclude from *Ps. Sol.* 18.16-18, after Pompey put Hyrcanus on the throne, that they might have fled into the desert.[149] In so doing, he presupposes, like many others, that the *Psalms of Solomon* are a Pharisaic writing,[150] for which, nevertheless, we find no more documentation than an identification of the representatives of the people.[151] Here also the reduction of the history of the Jews to a polarity of Pharisees and Sadducees seems a gross oversimplification.

3. UNDER HEROD

BJ 1.208-211 tells how the young Herod's successes in putting down the insurgents ("robbers") in Galilee aroused the envy of so many people at the court of Hyrcanus that Herod was finally brought

---

Moyne, *Les Sadducéens*, 92: "Pas plus que les descriptions de Josèphe, ce données du Qoumrân [that is, 4QpNah] ne permettent de faire l'équivalence entre Sadducéens et partisans d'Aristobule II."

149. G. Alon, *The Attitude*, 29.

150. Thus, for example, S. Holm-Nielsen, *Die Psalmen Salomos*, JSHRZ (Gütersloh, 1977), 59; "We cannot doubt that the *Psalms of Solomon* correspond with Pharisaic spiritual inclinations"; yet we may not interpret them "out of a strict Pharisaic dogmatism." Similarly, J. Schüpphaus, *Die Psalmen Salomos* (Leiden, 1977), 5–11, 127–37, interprets them "as a document from the early period of the Pharisee movement," which is otherwise hardly documented and does not correspond to the later, predominantly legalistically oriented Pharisaism (137). This argumentation is circular! R. R. Hann, *The Community*, is more careful. M. Lana offers a balanced portrayal of the problem in P. Sacchi (ed.), *Apocrifi dell'Antico Testamento* (Turin, 1989), 2:55–60.

151. The exaltation of Davidic rule in *Ps. Sol.* 17:4ff. in such a combination of sources leads frequently to the conclusion that the Pharisees were the principal opponents of the Hasmoneans, since the latter were not descendants of the house of David. This would presuppose a fundamental change in Pharisaic ideas from previously and cannot be documented.

to trial because he had, against the law of the Jews, killed so many people. Hyrcanus then acquitted Herod upon the recommendation of Sextus Caesar. *AJ* 14.171-76 amplifies this with a description of the appearance of Herod before the Synhedrion, fully clothed in royal purple and accompanied by his soldiers. The council members were mute. Only a certain man, "Samaias by name, [whom] he held in the greatest honor because of his uprightness," advised the council and the king to admit Herod, for God would one day punish them and the king through Herod. When Herod later came into power, he fulfilled this prophecy; he killed all of the members of the Synhedrion with the exception of Samaias. He also had great respect for Samaias because he later advised the people in the besieged city of Jerusalem to allow Herod in. Because of his sins he was unable to get away. A bit later Josephus takes this up again, but with some interesting changes. Along with those who had previously been for Herod,

> Especially honoured by him were Pollion the Pharisee and his disciple Samaias, for during the seige of Jerusalem these men had advised the citizens to admit Herod, and for this they now received their reward. This same Pollion had once, when Herod was on trial for his life, reproachfully foretold to Hyrcanus and the judges that if Herod's life were spared, he would (one day) persecute them all. And in time this turned out to be so, for God fulfilled his words. (*AJ* 15.3–4)

Thus Pollio replaces Samaias (see the text variant here). It is first here that the man is even identified as a Pharisee. It is a debatable point whether these two are the same as Abtalion and Shemaia (or Abtalion and Shammai) from the rabbinic tradition.[152] It is at least clear that a Pharisee is being mentioned as a member of the Sanhedrin under Hyrcanus II, and that he pleaded in a case with a death penalty. His prophetic gift demonstrated in this context and above

---

152. Uniquely, A Schalit, *König Herodes,* 768–71, derives Pollio from the Greek *polios,* 'grey,' thus identifying him as Hillel, "the old one," and the other as Shammai.

all his statements on Herod's behalf in the year 37 B.C.E., in any case, secured Herod's favor for him.

At least these two Pharisees were prepared to accept Herod's unavoidable rule. Were all of the other members of the Sanhedrin, whom Herod had executed (thus *AJ* 14.175 and 15.6 speak of 45 *protoi* of Antigonus's party), also Pharisees?[153] Josephus says nothing more; at most we might infer the continuation of the relationship under Salome Alexandra. Nevertheless, the Talmudic legend *b. B. Bat.* 3b seems to support this: Herod killed all of the rabbis, leaving only Baba ben Buta. This text would then support the Pharisees' rejection of Herod: he was not of Jewish heritage (see Deut. 17:15). The text is hardly usable from a historical perspective, especially since it is apparently closely linked with *b. Qidd.* 66a concerning the killing of the Pharisees by Alexander Jannaeus.[154] It is clear that many Pharisees, like Pollio and Samaias, would have preferred over Herod a Jew who was not descended from the house of David.[155]

When Herod instituted a tax reduction around the year 20 B.C.E. in order to win the people over to himself and in the process demanded an oath of loyalty, the Pharisees Pollio and Samaias and their pupils could resist with impunity, as did the Essenes (15.370f.), while other resisters were persecuted. *AJ* 17.41f. speaks again of the Pharisees' refusal to swear allegiance:[156] Herod penalized them (about 6,000 men) with a fine that was ultimately paid by Pheroras's wife. For that the Pharisees told her that her family would gain

---

153. J. Patrich, *A Sadducean Halakha*, 33, regards the 45 *protoi* to be Sadducees and believes that Herod held to the Pharisaic law with respect to the Temple construction.

154. J. Efron, *Studies*, 185. Compare also the scene of the young Herod before the *Synhedrion* with *b. Sanh.* 19a-b on the court case that Alexander Jannaeus leveled against Simeon ben Shetah, whose slave had killed a man (on this see Efron, 190ff.).

155. See A. Schalit, *König Herodes*, 98–101.

156. It is debatable (and not important for us) whether the same conflict is described twice (thus, for example, D. R. Schwarz, *Josephus*, 160), or whether two different refusals to swear alliance are described (thus, for example, A. J. Saldarini, *Pharisees*, 99, n. 53).

the throne of Herod. When Herod received this news, he had the guiltiest of the Pharisees and "those of his household who approved of what the Pharisee had said" (17.44) executed.[157]

Why did the Pharisees refuse to take the oath? If they rejected the idea that they were simultaneously supposed to swear allegiance to Caesar (17.42), were they opposed to Herod's rule or did they reject any oath out of principal? If the certainly tendentious characterization of Josephus or his source is supposedly correct—that the Pharisees promised the throne to Pheroras and his family—they could only be opposed to Herod, not against any Idumean ruler, as is usually generalized.[158] Unfortunately, Josephus gives us no further information.

The number 6,000 is interesting. Does it indicate the total number of Pharisees or just those who refused to take the oath? Or did all of the Pharisees refuse to swear? As always, if we are permitted to rely on its accuracy, this number shows that the Pharisees were a very small minority in the total Jewish population.

4. UP TO THE DESTRUCTION OF JERUSALEM

According to the usual interpretation, the Pharisees at the time of Herod had withdrawn from political life and had evolved from a

---

157. E. Rivkin, *A Hidden Revolution,* 321–24. This passage does not agree precisely with his picture of the Pharisees; among other things, the Pharisees are not designated as a *hairesis* but rather a *morion,* numbering only 6,000 members. Samaias and Pollio were exempt from the oath of loyalty. Apparently Rivkin regards this as the totality of the Pharisees. Here the Pharisees are also not represented as a group contrasting with the Sadducees. Thus, we must here understand *Pharisee* literally as "separatist, fanatic" and not as the *hairesis* of the Pharisees of which Josephus otherwise speaks. He uses the term with fidelity to his source. Everything argues against such a termination of power. Also, Josephus does not otherwise mention the Pharisees in parallel to each mention of the Sadducees. *Morion* in place of *hairesis* may go back to Josephus's version, but it may also simply indicate a "portion" of the Pharisees, who unlike Samaias and Pollio were not exempt from the oath. The idea that the number 6,000 may be much too low for the total membership of the Pharisees lacks any foundation.

158. See A. Schalit, *König Herodes,* 471–73.

political party to a movement that was concerned with spirituality,[159] for which the development of the schools of Hillel and Shammai would be symptomatic. The few citations of the Pharisees during the period of Herod that Josephus makes show indeed that they (or some of them) quite probably tried to take part in politics. To be sure, Josephus says that the two teachers in Jerusalem, who during Herod's final illness incited their students to tear the eagle down from the gate of the Temple and thus guarantee an insurrection, were not Pharisees. Nevertheless, their description as "experts who had a reputation for being very exact regarding the laws of their country" (*sophistai . . . malista dokountes akriboun ta patria; BJ* 1.648, compare *AJ* 17.241) is strongly reminiscent of the stereotypical descriptions of the Pharisees, whose *akribeia* is repeatedly emphasized. This at least suggests identifying them as Pharisees.[160]

When discussing the establishment of the "fourth philosophy" in 6 C.E., which was hostile to Rome, Josephus does mention explicitly that the Galilean Judas of Gamala was suppported by the Pharisee Zadok (*AJ* 17.3f.); only their indefatigable love of freedom and the fact the only leader and ruler that they would acknowledge was God distinguished them from the Pharisees (*AJ* 17.23). They apparently split with the Pharisees over the question of the acknowledgement of Roman rule; the more radical probably joined with groups of zealots or were at least prepared to support them again and again, while others attempted to achieve a modus vivendi with the ruling powers and withdrew ever further into the realm of inner spirituality.[161] The question asked by a few Pharisees and followers of Herod whether people ought to pay taxes to Caesar (Mark 12:13ff.) probably refers to the fact that at least some Pharisaic

159. Thus, for example, V. Tcherikover, *Hellenistic Civilization,* 253f., and especially J. Neusner, *From Politics to Piety.* "Evidently, the end of the Pharisaic party comes with Aristobolus, who slaughtered many of them, and was sealed by Herod, who killed even more" (J. Neusner, *Josephus' Pharisees,* 291). After that time as a group they ceased to play a role in the political life of Palestine.

160. Thus, for example, M. Hengel, *Die Zeloten,* 330f., in conjunction with H. Graetz, *Geschichte* 3:235, 797.

161. M. Hengel, *Die Zeloten,* 58f., 89–91.

circles rejected taxes to the Roman authorities, even if they had no practical consequences. It is also remarkable that Pharisees and Herodians were treated together in the Markan account: Is it possible that Pharisees, contrary to their normal opposition to the house of Herod, established a coalition with circles around Herod Antipas for some particular purposes? Mark presupposes a partial common interest between the two groups.[162]

Unfortunately, we have no explicit statements about the Pharisees from Josephus for the decades immediately preceding the outbreak of war against Rome and must rely entirely upon the New Testament; nevertheless, the silence of Josephus (whose information for the period between Herod and the outbreak of the rebellion is rather incomplete) ought not to be used together with biased New Testament and rabbinic traditions directly as arguments for the Pharisees' retreat from public life. A rejection of political life on principle is hardly conceivable; more likely there was a lack of possibility during the period of direct Roman rule.

Josephus's statements give us no more precise information about the spread of the Pharisees and Sadducees in a particular period, since he is primarily interested in political activity and especially relationships in Jerusalem. Are we to interpret what he has to say about the two groups exclusively as phenomena of the capital? The New Testament would seem to support this idea at least for the Sadducees, whose only confrontation with Jesus (according to Mark and Luke) was located in Jerusalem (the additional passages in Matthew are probably redactional). This fits with the usual interpretation of the Sadducees as a priestly party that was naturally concentrated around the Temple.[163]

---

162. For an attempt to identify the Herodians with one of the religious parties—the Sadducees or the Essenes—see H. W. Hoehner, *Herod Antipas,* 331–42. He, along with L. Finkelstein, equates them with the Boethusians, who were politically on Herod's side but theologically aligned with the Sadducees. C. Daniel attempts to identify the Herodians with the Essenes in a series of essays. For this, see W. Braun, "Were the NT Herodians Essenes?"

163. See, for example, G. Baumbach, *Jesus,* 51, who calls the Sadducees "the regular party of the higher Jerusalem priesthood."

We usually regard the Pharisees as centered in Jerusalem and Judea. This possibly fits with Mark 7:1. Nevertheless, the relative clause, "who had come from Jerusalem," is not necessarily associated with the Pharisees. In contrast, the practice in the Synoptics is to locate Jesus' conflicts with the Pharisees in Galilee; only the "taxes to Caesar" narrative is placed in Jerusalem (with the Herodians!).[164] The Gospels are in any case of limited use as proof for the spread of the Pharisaic movement in Galilee, since the redactional interests of Mark (the contrast of Galilee-Jerusalem) ought to be considered (they may have affected modifications also in Matthew and Luke). We learn practically nothing about the numeric strength or the influence of the Pharisees in Mark.[165] However, the friendly contacts between Jesus and the Pharisees in Galilee, as described by Luke (for example, the invitation in 11:37, the warning about Herod in 13:31), can probably be taken as evidence of isolated Pharisees in Galilee.[166] We cannot reject the idea that Paul might have been a Pharisee with a passing reference to the idea that there were no Pharisees in Asia Minor. We have no evidence for Pharisees in the Diaspora; nevertheless, a conclusion based on the incidental silence of the sources here is not reliable, even if the observance of various religious laws, especially those of ritual purity, must have been

164. D. Lührmann, *Die Pharisäer,* 180, considers this to be Markan redaction rather than an older tradition, while others derive all mention of the Pharisees in Mark from the tradition.

165. Lührmann, ibid., 181, regards the geographic differentiation in Mark (according to whom the Pharisees were the opponents of Jesus in Galilee, the scribes in Jerusalem) as evidence of Mark's redactional inclination: "At the time of Jesus there were apparently hardly any Pharisees left in Galilee." According to Lührmann the topics of discussion in the debates with the Pharisees were questions of *halakah,* which were no longer of actual interest for the Christian community. The scribes were the actual opponents of the Christian community.

166. U. Schnelle, *Jesus;* U. Luz, *Jesus,* 241, regards the significance of the Pharisees in Matthew (probably originating in Syria) as a possible reference to the geographical expansion of the influence of the Pharisees after 70 C.E. S. Freyne, *Galilee from Alexander the Great to Hadrian* (Wilmington, 1980), 319–23 surmises some dissemination of the Pharisees in the period before 70 C.E. especially around the Sea of Gennesaret; see also A. J. Saldarini, *Pharisees,* 291–95.

extremely difficult in the Diaspora. It is naturally also quite conceivable that Paul first came into contact with the Pharisaic movement in Jerusalem.[167] To utilize the Gospel accounts of Jesus' trial to describe the way the various powers in Judaism of those years related to each other is problematic. A common thesis advanced today is that a Sadducean (rump) Sanhedrin passed the sentence against Jesus, which the Romans then executed. From this, certain attitudes of the Sadducees of that period are often deduced: a political consideration of power with the "preeminence of national/patriotic and cultic/ritual over the ethical"; the effort "through skillful use of the . . . available possiblities to achieve relative autonomy and stability in the hieratic governmental order in the best interest of the Jewish people."[168] Since the text here is not talking about Sadducees, conclusions of that kind rest on a classification of all of the high priests as Sadducees. According to Acts 5 there was at least one Pharisee, Gamaliel, in the Sanhedrin, and he was able to convince them of his own opinion. According to Acts 23 the Sanhedrin was composed of Pharisees and Sadducees. Whether the membership in one particular group was relevant or whether membership in the Sanhedrin was determined by other factors, such as family, possessions, or function, is not mentioned.

It is with Ananus, who executed James, the brother of Jesus (*AJ* 20.200) that we first meet the only high priest who is expressly called a Sadducee, and who subsequently was active in the initial phase of the rebellion against Rome.[169] At the beginning of the insurrection, we also encounter Pharisees again at the forefront of public life in Jerusalem. Josephus tells how the leading Pharisees

---

167. See, for example, J. Becker, *Paul: Apostle to the Gentiles* (Louisville, 1993), 33–56.

168. G. Baumbach, *Das Sadduzäerverständnis,* 24, 37.

169. For the role of the Sadducees (more precisely, the high priestly families) in the rebellion, see H. Schwier, *Tempel und Tempelzerstörung* (Göttingen, 1989), 173ff. R. A. Horsley, "High Priests and the Politics of Roman Palestine," *JSJ* 17 (1986): 23–55, manages almost without mention of the Sadducees. Membership in the social stratum of the nobility was certainly more important than adherence to one particular school of religious thought.

advocated in vain a peaceful solution; on the other hand, Pharisees figured prominently in the leadership of the revolt. There was probably no unity within the ranks.[170] Whether we can distinquish the Pharisees, who were for peace, as representatives of the school of Hillel, from the opponents of war as followers of Shammai, must remain doubtful, since there are no extrarabbinical sources extant for the early period of these schools. Still, the later rabbinic tradition appears to have understood it this way when it interpreted the notice of the eighteen *halakot* in *Šabb.* 1.4 with regard to a bloody altercation between the two schools, in which the school of Shammai enforced a sharp separation from non-Jews (*y. Šabb.* 1.4, 3c).[171] The cancellation of offerings for Caesar can, of course, be viewed in connection with this tradition. Josephus described in his biography how prominent Pharisees were involved for a time in the leadership of the revolt, to which we already referred in the section on his tendencies. None of the leading groups of Judaism was satisfied with inner religiosity, the Jewish religious understanding was always realized in political life, however its strength varied according to the given circumstances.

170. M. Goodman, *The Ruling Class,* 209: membership in a religious party was apparently irrelevant in political questions. Furthermore, it should not be assumed that the Pharisees were united on political matters. See also S. J. D. Cohen, *Josephus,* 223.

171. For the eighteen *halakhot,* see M. Hengel, *Die Zeloten,* 204ff.; for additional literature, see S. J. D. Cohen, *Josephus,* 218, n. 73.

FOUR

ESSENES, PHARISEES, SADDUCEES

The goal of this chapter will not be to add one more to the innumerable reconstructions of the history of the Essenes. We will only attempt to outline briefly a few of the connections between the history of the Essenes and the histories of the Pharisees and the Sadducees.[172]

Despite his thorough description of the Essenes, Josephus presents us with hardly any information that we can evaluate historically.[173] The historical portrait of the Essenes is usually based on the archeology of Qumran and historical references to them in Qumran writings; it presupposes that the Qumran community was a part of the larger Essene movement. The settlement of Qumran by the Essenes occurred in the late second century B.C.E., but a series of manuscripts found in Qumran are paleographically older and date

---

172. For the *status quaestionis* see G. Vermes, *The Dead Sea Scrolls*; F. García Martínez, "Estudios qumránicos 1975–1985: Panorama crítico," *Estudios Biblicos* 45 (1987): 125–205, 361–402; 46 (1988): 325–74, 527–48; 47 (1989): 93–118, 225–67.

173. G. Vermes (Schürer et al., *History of the Jewish People,* 2:562) thinks that the portrait of the Essenes in *AJ* is dependent upon Philo or a common source. A. Lemaire, "L'enseignement essénien et l'école de Qumrân," in *Hellenica et Judaica: Hommage à V. Nikiprowetzky* (Louvain-Paris, 1986), 191–203, 193, presupposes a much more direct knowledge of the Essenes. He suggests that Josephus, after his Saducean youth, might have had direct or indirect association with the Essenes up to the war. This may account for the fact that he never exercised his priestly office; J. Le Moyne refers to this in *Les Sadducéens,* 44.

back into the third century. Some of them, such as the fragments of
1 Enoch, the *Psalms of Joshua*,[174] and possibly also the *Temple
Scroll* may go back to pre-Essene times and were simply adopted
by the Essenes into their literature. Nevertheless, other texts such as
the Damascus document (CD) also suggest a longer prehistory,[175]
perhaps in Babylon, to which some Essene traditions could refer.[176]

1. THE HASMONEAN PERIOD

In general, CD 1.1-11 serves as a chronological starting point. This
portion of the text, probably belonging to a late stratum of the
whole of CD, speaks of the remnant in Israel, whom God spared
and remained with for 390 years after he handed them over to
Nebuchadnezzar; God caused a root to spring from the settlement
of Israel and Aaron and brought forth a Teacher of Righteousness
after twenty years of confusion. The number 390 is probably taken
from Ezek. 4:5 and should not be pressed further. Twenty might
also indicate about half a generation. We might get more precise
dates from the evidence about the teacher's opponents, namely the
wicked priests. We read about them in 1QpHab 8.8-13 that

> . . . the Wicked Priest . . . was called by the name of truth when he
> first arose. But when he ruled over Israel his heart became proud,
> and he forsook God and betrayed the precepts for the sake of riches.
> He robbed and amassed riches of the men of violence who rebelled
> against God, and he took the wealth of the peoples, heaping sinful
> iniquity upon himself. And he lived in the ways of abominations
> amidst every unclean defilement.

174. C. Newsom, "The 'Psalms of Joshua' from Qumran Cave 4," *JJS* 39
(1988): 56–73; cf. 68ff. for the overlapping with 4QTest 21–29, which is usually
associated with Simon the Maccabee.

175. On the thesis that CD was a pre-Essene writing that was later adopted and
reworked by the Essenes, see P. R. Davies, *The Damascus Covenant* (Sheffield,
1983).

176. See J. Murphy-O'Connor, *The Essenes and Their History.*

Most often Jonathan Maccabeus is identified as the figure behind the wicked priest, and most of the various references in the Qumran literature fit quite plausibly with this, even if other suggestions have been made, from Judas Maccabeus to Alexander Jannaeus.[177] Jonathan was at the head of the Jewish people beginning in 160 B.C.E.; in 152 Alexander Balas offered him the office of high priest; in 150 he was named strategist of Judah.

The decisive action for the founding of the community—the murder of the high priest Onias III in the year 172 B.C.E.—could have occurred within this time period. We might view the appearance of the teacher in conjunction with the assumption of the high priesthood by Jonathan in the year 152.[178] J. Murphy-O'Connor interprets the appearance of the community in CD as their migration from Babylon to Palestine, which he would like to support with the victories of the Maccabees starting in 165. However, he connects the appearance of the teacher with the events of 152. He suggests that the teacher might have been a Zadokite, who in the years up to 152 may have unofficially filled the role of high priest and in so doing was supported by the Essenes. After his displacement, he took over the leadership of the Essene community and with the nucleus of that group moved near the Dead Sea. This reconstruction is quite plausible, yet in its particulars it remains unprovable.

From this chronology or a somewhat earlier one it is not a large step to the Hasidean theory, which also dominates the reconstruction of the history of the Pharisees. Supporting a connection with the *Chasidim* is the name of the Essenes, which—along with other

177. Not every mention of a wicked priest in the Qumran texts necessarily refers to the same person. See, especially, W. H. Brownlee, *The Wicked Priest*, as well as A. S. van der Woude, *Wicked Priest*. Brownlee, *The Wicked Priest,* 18ff., and *The Midrash Pesher,* 95ff., associates this passage with John Hyrcanus, who also according to rabbinic tradition (*Ber.* 29a) was still good at the beginning.

178. An earlier estimated date is advocated, for example, by B. Z. Wacholder, *The Dawn of Qumran* (Cincinnati, 1983), 181ff., who dates the beginning of the community to 196–195 and the triumph of the teacher to 177–176. His opponent might have been the high priest Simeon the Righteous. For F. García Martínez, Judas Maccabeus was the counterpoint to the teacher.

attempts at explanation—is often derived from *ḥasid*[179] or the Greek equivalent *hosios*.[180] It is indeed attractive to see in the Essenes or their predecessors the people who, according to 1 Macc. 1:29, withdrew to caves in the desert and allowed themselves to be killed on the Sabbath without a fight; nevertheless, as we have already seen, that passage does not form a single unit with 1:42ff., where the topic under discussion is the Hasideans; therefore, the two groups are not to be equated. The three explicit statements in the books of Maccabees about the Hasideans do not allow us to conclude that they were a self-contained movement, which after the Maccabean revolt divided into the Pharisees and the Essenes. Since we are not able with certainty to deal with the Pharisees as a historical reality in the second century, it is also true that we cannot reconstruct a common prehistory for the two movements directly; at most, we can do so for the history of their ideas.

CD 1:12ff. speaks of a community of betrayers; the "scoffer" has poured lies over Israel. They sought the "smooth things" (*daršu ba-ḥalaqot*), chose deception, and violated the covenant. In 4QpNah the *dorše ha-ḥalaqot* are equated with the Pharisees with relative ease; for that reason we might here also think of them and see in the Pharisees a group that has fallen away from common ideals and under the influence of the "scoffer." The "builders of the wall" (*bone ha-ḥayyis*), against whom the CD raises polemic (4.19, 8.12, 18 [= 19.24, 31]), is a good parallel for the Pharisees.[181] The designation ascribed to them (first attested for the rabbis in *m. ʾAbot* 1.1)

179. R. Meyer, s.v. "pharisaios," *TWNT* 9.14, sees direct evidence in a fragment from Muraba'at (DJD 2:163), which mentions a *meṣad ḥasidin*. The term, however, is too general.

180. For this, see Philo, *Quod omnis probus*, 75. To attempt to connect the name with the institution found especially in Ephesus, the *essēnia*, see J. Kampen, *The Hasideans*, 172ff., and A. H. Jones, *Essenes: The Elect of Israel and the Priests of Artemis* (Lanham, 1985).

181. See, for example, J. M. Baumgarten, *Studies*, 33: "The false ruling of the Pharisaic 'builders of fences'"; R. Meyer, *TWNT* 9:30f. Keen on developing a hypothesis, H. Burgmann, "Der Gründer der Phariäergenossenschaft: Der Makkabäer Simon," *JSJ* 9 (1978): 153–91, develops this thesis.

comes from a fence around the Torah. Nevertheless, in CD 1 it is not certain which period the polemic addresses. The formulation "smooth teaching" does not necessarily always mean in every place the same group of people, but simply accuses them of being enemies, who interpret the Torah in too easy a fashion. Ephraim, who also separated itself from Judah (CD 7.12f.), should not be regarded as the splitting of the Essenes from the Pharisees as is often done.[182] If the polemical statements in CD are to be interpreted factually as a traumatic break at the beginning of the movement, that would not necessarily have been the dismemberment of a hypothetical Hasidic community of similarly minded people into the Pharisees and Essenes. We might just as easily interpret the polemical statements of CD as a break within the Essene community itself, wherein the polemic was between the group who left Jerusalem with the teacher and the rest (probably the majority), who were ready to compromise and consequently were accused of "seeking to avoid roughness."[183] Such a view can indeed be combined with the common perception—that the laws of CD might have been intended for the Essenes scattered throughout the country and not for the community of Qumran—by means of a complex literary history of origin.

W. H. Brownlee would connect 1QpHab 5.8-12 with the narrative of Hyrcanus's banquet for the Pharisees in *AJ* 13.290-92 and *b. Qidd.* 66a:

> "O traitors, why do you stare and stay silent when the wicked man swallows up the one who is more righteous than he?" (1:13b)
>
> Interpreted, this concerns the House of Absalom and the members of its council who were silent at the time of the chastisement of the Teacher of Righteousness and gave him no help against the Liar who flouted the Law in the midst of their whole [congregation.] (1QpHab 5.8-12)

---

182. With J. Murphy-O'Connor, *The Essenes*, 241, Ephraim is rather to be regarded as a designation of all who opposed the group of the Teacher of Righteousness for religious reasons (244: "the whole of non-Qumran Judaism").

183. Thus J. Murphy-O'Connor, *The Essenes*, 233ff.

Accordingly, the Pharisee Eleazar was described by Josephus as someone of bad character who demanded that Hyrcanus renounce the high priesthood, the Teacher of Righteousness, who in the discussion of the "house of Absalom," the Pharisees, was left alone. The Essenes would accordingly be simply the radical wing of the Pharisees.[184] The Essenes' break with Jerusalem in the later Hyrcanus period would be without problem from the archaeological evidence from Qumran, but the text is too general to be able to be identified specifically with this situation.

Brownlee's historical interpretation of the Habakkuk pesher's continuation is even more problematic. 11.8-17 describes the death of the wicked priest, who here might be identified with Jannaeus. After his attack on Qumran on the Day of Atonement of the Essenes (11.2-8), they took revenge on him: 11.17–12.10 might be connected with the episode in *AJ* 13.372f., where the people pelted Jannaeus with citrons on the Festival of Tabernacles. The unrest may have been resolved by the Essenes, who now again had found the support of the Pharisees. Unfortunately, the gaps in our historical knowledge are not so easily filled. The story of the religious parties, as we know it from Josephus, can be connected with Qumran texts only in the rarest of cases (thus in 4QpNah).[185]

If we do not set the departure of the people around the teacher as late as Brownlee, we cannot exclude a settlement of the Essenes yet under Jonathan on the basis of archeology, rather we might consider a longer phase of irregular wandering, or we might regard the exile in Damascus, which CD mentions frequently, as the beginning. It is debatable whether Damascus is to be taken literally or symbolically; Qumran itself could hardly be intended, since they left Judah for Damascus (CD 6.5), and Qumran lies within Judah.

Around 100 B.C.E. active construction was begun on an expansion of the buildings and the water supply. Does this indicate the

---

184. W. H. Brownlee, *The Midrash Pesher,* 93, 95–97, and Brownlee, *The Wicked Priest,* 18ff.; 1QpHab reflects "a time of agreement between the Pharisees and the Sadducees to persecute the Righteous Teacher" (26).

185. However, A. J. Saldarini, *Pharisees,* 278–80, correctly warns here against a too hasty identification of the enemies as the Pharisees.

beginning of the Essene settlement or the addition of new members? J. T. Milik connected these changes with the persecution of the Pharisees toward the end of the reign of John Hyrcanus, suggesting that many Pharisees joined the Qumran community; a portion of them might have gone back toward Damascus or southern Syria, influencing the regulations set down in the Damascus document. Its prescriptions on family life, ritual purity, and Sabbath rest might be "hallmarks that illustrate the rather Pharisaic tendencies of the new group in Damascus."[186] That there should be not only a priest as leader, as in Qumran, but also a lay leader at the head of the community, points also to the Pharisaic influence, as does the development of the messianic teaching, which at this stage also had room for one who "had been royally anointed." Under Alexander Jannaeus the influx of the Pharisees increased.

As attractive as this reconstruction might appear on first glance, it should be regarded with care. The date and classification of the Damascus document in the Essene movement is quite uncertain, but also the archeological evidence is not so clear and might suggest that not until around 100 did a larger group of Essenes settle in Qumran or find the means to undertake a comprehensive building program.[187] Likewise the persecution of the Pharisees under John Hyrcanus is not entirely certain, as we have already seen. Pharisaic immigration under Jannaeus would be easier to substantiate. Nevertheless, how typical were the characteristics listed by Milik, especially for a Pharisaic influence upon the group? The Sabbath was already extremely important in the *Temple Scroll*; prescriptions for

---

186. J. Milik, *Die Geschichte,* 108ff.; quote from p. 111. In DJD 6 (1977) Milik published *tefillin* and *mezuzot* from Qumran among which were "Pharisaic types" (47) from around the beginning of the first century, which he does not connect explicitly with the influx of the Pharisees in Qumran. This, however, is probably done by J. H. Charlesworth, *The Origin,* 244, following Milik's earlier thesis.

187. See especially E.-M. Laperrousaz, "Brèves remarques archéologique concernant la chronologie des occupations esséniennes de Qoumrân," *RQ* 12 (1986): 199–212 (summary of *Qoumrân: L'établissement essénian des bords de la Mer Morte* [Paris, 1976]).

ritual purity accord quite well with priestly concerns; finally, the expectation of a royal messiah is attested quite clearly in the *Psalms of Solomon*, which are not as easy to assign to the Pharisees as is often done. Here also we see the difficulty in making a clean division of the Judaism of that period into Pharisees, Sadducees, and Essenes.

We would also have to consider how in such a hypothetical immigration of the Pharisees to Qumran, which indeed presupposes a corresponding spiritual kinship, we can accommodate a persecution of the Qumran community by the Pharisees shortly thereafter, during the time of Salome Alexandra, as the Pesher Nahum is usually interpreted.

2. UNDER HEROD

The period of Herod is of greatest interest for our study. On the basis of the excavations, R. de Vaux has concluded that the settlement of Qumran was destroyed by an earthquake in 31 B.C.E. and only after the death of Herod in 4 B.C.E. was it rebuilt, existing then without interruption until 68 C.E. Archeological evidence for an exodus from the settlement at this time is not quite conclusive,[188] yet it seems probable that there was at least a little bit of activity by the Essenes in Qumran during this phase. We are compelled to ascribe the Qumran manuscripts, which are paleographically dated in the Herodian period, to the few remaining Essenes or to their followers, who were dispersed throughout the country.

Josephus wrote that Herod pardoned the Essenes out of loyalty and accorded them great honor, since while he was still a child he was greeted by Manaemus as king of the Jews. This fulfilled prophecy caused him to value the Essenes quite highly (*AJ* 15.371-79).

---

188. See P. R. Callaway, *The History,* 37ff.: ten Herodian coins have been found at Qumran. J. H. Charlesworth, *The Origin,* 225f., prefers to connect the destruction of Qumran with the Parthian invasion of the years 40–37 B.C.E. E.-M. Laperrousaz, "Brèves remarques," 208, thinks that Pompey's conquest in 67 B.C.E. may have already led to desertion of the settlement, which was reinhabited from 24 B.C.E. onward.

Josephus did not tell us how the Essenes reacted to Herod's cooperation or how and when he interacted with Essenes—apart from Manaemus. His route from Jericho to Masada must have led him past Qumran repeatedly, and he might likewise have had contact with the Essene communities scattered throughout the countryside. C. Daniel certainly exaggerated when he equates the Essenes with the Herodians,[189] yet the Herodian period was certainly a turning point in the history of the Essenes.

Since Qumran was apparently more or less uninhabited during Herod's reign, the most important information about the Essenes who were scattered throughout Israel are briefly summarized here. This is not to say that the relevant texts relate just to this period, yet they treat the great majority of the Essenes and were therefore especially relevant.

The discoveries at Qumran have diverted attention away from the Essene groups who, according to Philo and Josephus, were not located by the Dead Sea but were found in all of the cities of Palestine. Here Josephus is probably speaking about his own time. Why, then, did the authors of the New Testament not mention the Essenes? According to Josephus's figures, the Essenes had about 4,000 members (*AJ* 18.20; likewise Philo, *Quod omnis probus,* 75), which is a figure not much smaller than the figure 6,000 that he gave for the Pharisees under Herod.

The Essenes, whom Josephus mentions by name, were probably not all in Qumran but rather lived in Jerusalem. Thus it was with the Essene Judah who, together with numerous students, lived in or near the temple in Jerusalem. Judah had foretold the death of Antigonus (103 B.C.E.) in Strato's tower, but he incorrectly connected this with Caesarea Maritima rather than Jerusalem (*BJ* 1.78-80).[190]

---

189. See the works of C. Daniels in the bibliography. Yadin, *The Temple Scroll,* 1:138f., believes that through a comparison of the *Temple Scroll* with Mark 8:14ff. (seven baskets of bread) this can be solidified, yet this contact cannot be proved.

190. J. Carmignac, "Qui était le Docteur de Justice?" *RQ* 10 (1979–81): 235–46, regards Judah as the Teacher of Righteousness. On the other hand, see J. Murphy-O'Connor, "Judah the Essene and the Teacher of Righteousness," ibid., 235–36.

It is not said where Herod met Menaemus, nor where Simon the Essene prophesied to Herod's son Archelaus the early end of his reign (*BJ* 2.113). Both events could have taken place in Jerusalem. We might also imagine Josephus's examination of the Essene teachings to have happened there, insofar as we are able to rely upon his own statements. The fourth Essene mentioned by Josephus is John, who in the Jerusalem temple was made commander of the rebellion in the district of Thamna, but who also was over Lydda, Jaffa, and Emmaus (*BJ* 2.567).

In his description of the Essenes, Josephus had the members who were dispersed throughout the country and not those who were living in Qumran.[191] According to *BJ* 2.124, there were Essenes living in all of the cities of Palestine (compare Philo, *Apology* 1; on the other hand *Quod omnis probus* 76 states that they avoided the cities and lived in villages). They led a communal life and had their own dining rooms, to which nonmembers were not admissable, but traveling Essenes were invited to meals (129, 132). There were also married members among them (160f.). This evidence coincides with information in the Damascus document and the addendum to the community regulations 1QSa, which both mention married members and the relation of the community to non-Jews (or nonmembers). 4Q159 also hardly belongs at the center of Qumran.[192] J. Murphy-O'Connor believes that reference in CD to non-Jewish surroundings allows us to conclude that it came from the time of the community's diaspora, but these statements fit equally well in Palestine, which was, at least regionally, densely populated with Gentiles; moreover, we may conclude from the late copies in Qumran that the text remained relevant.

Determinations regarding relationships with non-Jews in CD 12.6-11 have, for the most part, Tannaitic parallels[193] and indicate a

---

191. For Josephus's text, see especially, T. S. Beall, *Josephus' Description*.

192. F. D. Weinert, "4Q159: Legislation for an Essene Community outside of Qumran?" *JSJ* (1974): 179–207.

193. See L. H. Schiffman, "Legislation Concerning Relations with Non-Jews in the Zadokite Fragments and in Tannaitic Literature," *RQ* 11 (1983): 379–89.

broader, common basis for the Judaism of that period. It is note-worthy that in such a legalistic community it was necessary to forbid shedding the blood of a non-Jew just to obtain his property. Similarly, Josephus (*BJ* 2.141f.) stated that the Essenes promise to keep their hands from larceny and goods dishonestly gained, but also from robbery (*lēsteia*). It would be attractive to connect *lēsteia*, in line with Josephus's customary usage, with political rebellion, especially taking part in guerilla action. Shortly before, in 2.140, he also stated that the Essenes promised to defend the trust of the authorities, since no one becomes a ruler apart from God.[194] That would enable an unstrained relationship with Herod's government, and then there would have been no point of conflict with him over the high priesthood.

The *Copper Scroll* from Qumran might contain concrete refer-ences to Essene communities. If this text actually comes from Es-sene circles and indicates real hiding places—in other words, is not pure fiction—we might conclude with B. Pixner that the hiding places described there were under the control of Essene groups or at least were easily accessible to them.[195] The 64 places mentioned are, insofar as we can determine, in the vicinity of Jerusalem, around Jericho, and in the Yarmuk Region. It would be enticing to see a reference to the spreading of the Essenes.[196]

We must refer here especially to the "Essene Gate" in Jerusalem mentioned by Josephus, which we might be successful in finding if we go westward from the tower of Hippicus (the modern Jaffa Gate) past the place called Bethso (*BJ* 5.142-45). If we interpret the term *Bethso* as a transliteration of the Hebrew *bet ṣo'ah,* 'latrine,'

---

194. Attempts to connect this to the leader of the Essene community (thus, for example, T. S. Beall, *Josephus' Description,* 80f.) are not quite convincing.

195. B. Pixner, "Unravelling the Copper Scroll Code: A Study of the Topogra-phy of 3Q15," *RQ* 11 (1982–84): 323–65. The term *koḥlit* frequently mentioned in the text is interesting; it calls to mind the campaign against Koḥlit by Yannai after which there was the fateful banquet with the Pharisees (*b. Qidd.* 66a).

196. C. Daniel, *Les Esséniens,* 273, interprets the statements of *m. Pesaḥ.* 4.8 and *b. Pesaḥ.* 55b-56a on the the people of Jericho as a polemic against the Essenes, who, however, would hardly have affirmed the same customs.

we can connect this with the regulations in the *Temple Scroll*, according to which Jerusalem ought not to be polluted by excrement. Thus they had to construct a latrine 3,000 cubits northwest of the city (11QT 46.13-16). From there it is usually posited that the Essene Gate was in the vicinity of the modern Gate of Zion.[197] Even if the excavations lead by B. Pixner cannot be unequivocally classified with the Essenes, we may assume that the Essene Gate refers to an Essene community that lived in the vicinity of this gate and perhaps used it for access to the latrine. But the question remains unclear to what extent the *Temple Scroll* offers a rather utopian program, and where it influenced actual conditions. In any case, this aspect of the laws of ritual purity conforms to the information in *BJ* 2.148f.[198]

This would mean that the Jerusalem Essenes remain in the city, even if they are convinced that the other residents are polluting the city with their behavior. Likewise, the Essenes appear to accept the Temple, even if the cult practiced there and the calendar followed there do not correspond to their ideals. In the beginning, much was concluded on the basis of the criticism of the Temple in the Qumran texts, often the complete rejection of the Temple, the construction of ersatz rites in Qumran,[199] or a cult exclusively devoted to sacrifice, even if the excavations show no indication of an altar. Apparently, over the course of time, the complete rejection of the Jerusalem Temple, which was regarded as defiled (CD 4.18; 5.6f. defilement through not observing laws regarding menstruation, 1QpHab 12.7-9), made room for a variety of opinions,[200] which

197. Thus Y. Yadin, "The Gate of the Essenes and the Temple Scroll," in *Jerusalem Revealed: Archeology and the Holy City 1968–1974* (Jerusalem, 1975), 90f.; Yadin, *The Temple Scroll* 1:301–4, following him is B. Pixner, "An Essene Quarter on Mount Zion," in *Studia Hierosolymitana,* FS B. Bagatti (Jerusalem, 1976), 245–84, who believes that he has found the remains of the Essene quarter outside the Gate of Zion in the Protestant cemetery.

198. See T. S. Beall, *Josephus' Description,* 97–99.

199. See C. Newsom, *Songs of the Sabbath Sacrifice: A Critical Edition* (Atlanta, 1985), 61ff.

200. J. Murphy-O'Connor, *The Essenes,* 237, believes that in the early period the Essenes who had not moved to Qumran boycotted the Temple, because the

even enabled the sending of votive gifts to the Temple. CD 6.11-20, which is often interpreted as an absolute rejection of the Temple, could also be regarded as the disowning of a cult that was being improperly executed:

> None of those brought into the covenant shall enter the Temple to light his altar in vain. They shall bar the door, forasmuch as God said, "Who among you will bar its door?" (Mal 1:10). They shall take care to act according to the exact interpretation of the Law during the age of wickedness. They shall separate from the sons of the Pit, and shall keep away from the unclean riches of wickedness acquired by vow or anathema or from the Temple treasure; they shall not rob the poor of His people, to make of widows their prey and of the fatherless their victim (Isa 10:2). They shall distinguish between clean and unclean, and shall proclaim the difference between holy and profane. They shall keep the Sabbath day according to its exact interpretation. . . ." (CD 6.11-20)[201]

So long as the cult functioned in accordance with the correct Essene calendar, the correct understanding of ritual purity, and other ideas regarding sacrifice, there was apparently no objection to the Temple, but the door remained open for a later reevaluation of the cult and a new interpretation. This is in accord with Josephus (*AJ* 18.19):

> They send votive offerings to the temple, but perform their sacrifices employing a different ritual of purification. For this reason they are

---

followers of the man of lies were never charged with a cultic offense. "Had the members of the non-Qumran branch continued to frequent the Temple, they would surely have been accused of cultic faults as was the Wicked Priest."

201. A. I. Baumgarten, *The Name,* 420f., suggests that the *ke-peruš* emphasized in CD 6.14, 18, 20 underscores the claim of the Essenes that they themselves are the *parošim,* the ones who interpret the Torah precisely, not the Pharisees, who simplify the Torah as *dorše ḥalaqot* (1.18f.). As plausible as that sounds, nevertheless, the terms are too general to say this with certainty. In addition, dating the texts would be essential for a more precise interpretation.

barred from those precincts of the temple that are frequented by all the people and perform their rites by themselves.[202]

The statement that they offer sacrifice in the Temple (*epitelousin*) does not necessarily mean that the priests of the Essenes killed the animals and brought the prescribed portions to the altar. Because of the different festival calendars, sacrifices for the feasts would be excluded in any case. We ought, rather, to think of individuals who make a voluntary sacrifice not bound by any limitation. Perhaps the Essenes went to the Temple to eat the portions of the sacrifice that belonged to the one who made the sacrifice (thus *epitelousin* also in the narrower sense of completing the sacrifice), and they went back in another area of the Temple, where they would be by themselves.[203]

The "consecrated gifts" (*anathemata*) are probably to be interpreted primarily as the half shekel, which according to the opinion of Qumran in 4Q159,[204] was not to be made annually but only once during a person's lifetime.[205]

It is nearly impossible to give a more exact temporal order to the various statements regarding the Temple and sacrifice. On the one hand, it may be that the Essenes who were dispersed throughout the country had an attitude toward the Temple that was different from

202. The Latin text adds a negation: they offer *no* sacrifice. The Greek manuscripts, however, omit this. For the interpretation of this text, see T. S. Beall, *Josephus' Description,* 115–19.

203. Thus J. M. Baumgarten, *Studies,* 62ff. Even the *bet hishtachavot* of CD 11.22, which only a person who is ritually clean may enter, could be the Temple and not some eating place of the Essenes.

204. For this cf. J. Strugnell, *RQ* 7 (1969–71): 177. 4Q519 and 11QT 39.8f. also speak of the half shekel. In neither is the uniqueness made explicit. For this question, see also W. Stenger, "Geb dem Kaiser, was des Kaisers ist . . . !" (Frankfurt, 1988), 171ff., and S. Mandell, "Who Paid the Temple Tax When the Jews Were under Roman Rule?" *HTR* 77 (1984): 223–32.

205. Perhaps this is connected with the interpretation, ascribed to the Sadducees in *Men,* 65a, that the daily sacrifice can be made by an individual and does not have to be paid out of the Temple treasury. If the half shekel were only paid once, the Temple would probably not have had sufficient funds for the payment of the sacrifice.

those who were living at Qumran. They recognized at least to a certain extent the Temple in its actual character and accepted with it, somehow, the official festival calendar. On the other hand, it is possible that there was an attempted compromise during the Herodian period, and with the end of the Hasmonean high priests, perhaps even the Qumran Essenes joined the Temple, the ones who recognized as legitimate high priests the family of Boethos, who were in office from 24 B.C.E. They may have at least attempted to give up their isolation in the hope that they would have an easier time with their calendar and regulations regarding cleanliness.[206]

If we might assume that the Essenes of this period attempted to find some kind of unity with the high priests from the house of Boethos, it would also be conceivable that they were regarded by "everyday opinion" as a single group with the Sadducees or Boethusians. This would, perhaps, be an effort to explain not only the silence in the New Testament and rabbinic literature but also the rabbinic statements regarding the Sadducees and Boethusians, whose *halakic* views have been found only in Qumran. Then it would be easier to understand: the conflict over the festival calendar with the attempt to enforce their own point of view, the discussion of which cultic activities were to be permitted on the Sabbath, how the daily sacrifice was to be financed, the suspicion of those on the other side of not being precise enough in matters of ritual purity—all of these were points of conflict between the Essenes and the official cult, which were always ascribed rabbinically to the Sadducees or the Boethusians. Certainly, for many points we can cite common priestly *halakah*, yet it is hardly conceivable that Sadducean priests, for as long as they were in power in the Temple,

206. C. Daniel, *Nouveaux Arguments,* 399, considers the possibility that a substantial part of the priests who participated in the reconstruction of the Temple under Herod could have been Essenes who were accustomed to manual labor. But here again we are in the realm of hypothesis. However, J. Maier, "The Architectural History of the Temple in Jerusalem in the Light of the Temple Scroll," in *Temple Scroll Studies,* ed. G. J. Brooke (Sheffield, 1989), 25–62 has worked out a few places of correspondence between the Herodian Temple and 11QT (50–52).

were dependent upon the agreement of the Pharisees. In a period during which a compromise was again sought, we could imagine that many of these discussions would have taken place. Even the rabbinic narrative about Hillel, who first had to demonstrate that it was permissible to slaughter the Passover lamb even if the four-teenth of Nisan fell on a Sabbath (*t. Pesaḥ.* 4.13, Lieberman 165f.), gains a plausible context here. The regularly recurring and for that reason also long since resolved problem had to be completely ex-plained again for the benefit of the Essenes.

Of course, we are still in the realm of hypothesis here, which, however, can explain at least a few of the aspects of the history of the various branches of Judaism that are otherwise quite hard to understand. The historical heart of the story of *ʾAbot de Rabbi Nathan* might lie in the fact that after Herod the groups of priests and their followers, who had been united for a time, broke apart again into Zadokites, who returned again to Qumran, and Boethusians, who remained associated with the high priestly family and the Tem-ple. Or ought we to follow the suggestion of Azariah dei Rossi from the sixteenth century, who understood the Boethusians as *bet Issi' im*,[207] as the "house of the Essenes," who separated themselves from the followers of Zadok, the Sadducees? Of course, these are nothing more than theories, but they ought to be considered.

3. THE ESSENES AND
THE INSURRECTION AGAINST ROME

Philo described the Essenes as a peace-loving group who renounced the use of weapons (*Quod omnis probus* 78). In contrast, Josephus wrote not only that they took weapons along when they traveled (*BJ* 2.125), but also that they resisted steadfastly under the pressure of Roman torture (*BJ* 2.125f.). We have already seen that at least one Essene took part as a leader in the insurrection against Rome.

---

207. See Y. M. Grintz, "Die Männer des Yahad—Essener" (Hebrew). *Sinai* 32 (1953): 11–43, 42f. (the passage is missing in the German version in A. Schalit, ed. *Josephus Studien* [Darmstadt, 1973], 294–336); M. D. Herr, *Who Were the Boethu-sians?* 5.

The fact that Qumran manuscripts were also found in Masada likewise causes us to think that there were Essenes who participated in
the war against Rome. The Essenes have demonstrated themselves
not to have been complete pacifists; they were like the Hasideans
who were quite prepared to fight for the law with weapon in hand
(1 Macc. 2:42-48). 1QSa 1.21 establishes that even for the
eschatological community, no unqualified person may enter in order to assume a position in the war to overthrow the Gentiles.
Whether they interpreted the rebellion—in view of their military
role—as the eschatological struggle of the light against the dark-
ness, or they simply now saw the opportunity to purify the Temple
according to their interpretation of the law, we do not know. That,
however, the Pharisees and Sadducees, the Essenes and the zealots
found themselves ready to form a single community of action—
however brittle—with a common purpose in mind during the insurrection, demonstrates that they felt themselves ever more part of a
single Israel that transcended party boundaries.

FIVE

AFTER 70 c.e.:
BREAK OR CONTINUITY?

According to the commonly held view of all of the branches of Judaism, only the Pharisees survived the catastrophe of the year 70 c.e., passing seamlessly into the rabbinate. For this reason we often hear reference to "Pharisaic-rabbinic Judaism." The statement of C. Thoma, for example, is useful: "Rabbinism is Pharisaism that has been drawn out of a group existence and into responsibility for all of Judaism."[208]

Actually, the rabbinic texts suggest to the reader an impression of a Judaism that was unified under the rabbinate, that successfully overcame the party splintering of the period before 70. Soon Sadducees or Boethusians no longer appear in rabbinic literature as contemporaries of the rabbis, and Essenes are not mentioned at all. Occasional attempts to conclude that there was continued existence of the Sadducees on into the second century begin to collapse in the light of textual criticism, as well as the many anachronisms contained within these statements. The rabbis were acquainted with a divergent *halakah* of the Sadducees or Boethusians that we are today unable to distinguish from that of the people of Qumran. Insofar as the *halakah* points of conflict relate to the Temple, we could see a purely historical interest in their mention—propaganda for the victory of one's own ideas. The rabbinate appears to have made the claim to represent Judaism alone and without competition.

---

208. C. Thoma, *Der Pharisäismus*, 270.

S. J. D. Cohen formulates this impression in this way: "Jewish society from the end of the first century until the rise of the Karaites, was not torn by sectarianism."[209]

Only the appearance of the Karaites in the eighth century, whose ideas were partially related to Essene or Sadducean concepts, distorted the idyll of complete harmony under rabbinic leadership. If we can explain these parallels without historic dependence, they are at least partially transmitted by literary material (early Qumran discoveries)—or do they refer to a resistance, intensifying over the centuries, to rabbinic interpretations, which could be articulated more clearly only in the context of an Islamic world? We cannot take a closer look at these dilemmas here,[210] yet we should be warned against a one-dimensional reading of rabbinic texts.

How can we establish according to the early rabbinic texts that it was really the Pharisees that we find behind Judaism? The fact that the Pharisees increase in importance in the later Gospels and that simultaneously, Josephus accents the Pharisees much more in the *Jewish Antiquities* (*AJ*) than he did in the earlier *Jewish War* (*BJ*), suggests that the Pharisees increasingly dominated the scene after 70 c.e., and evolved into the rabbinate. This solution is certainly attractive, but could there not be other reasons behind this development? For example, the fact that the early Christian communities were especially involved in disputes with the Pharisees could mean that the traditions of the Pharisees also played a role in their own circles. Josephus could also have had personal reasons for the shift

209. S. J. D. Cohen, *The Significance,* 36. He considers Jabne's greatest contribution to Jewish history to be "the creation of a society which tolerates disputes without producing sects. For the first time Jews 'agreed to disagree'" (p. 29). This picture is in any case too harmonious, since it overlooks the great majority of the Jews, who remained outside of the rabbinic movement for a long time and were simply silenced by it, but they are becoming better known again because of archeological excavations in Israel.

210. For this, see A. Paul, *Écrits de Qumran et sectes juives aux premiers siècles de l'Islam* (Paris, 1969); B. Chiesa and W. Lockwood, *Ya'aqub al Qirqisani on Jewish Sects and Christianity* (Frankfurt, 1984); H. Ben Shammai, "Some Methodological Notes Concerning the Relationship Between the Karaites and Ancient Jewish Sects" (Hebrew), *Cathedra* 42 (1987): 69-84.

in his portrayal. Unfortunately, we know too little to be able to explain this remarkable agreement of Josephus and the Gospels in a conclusive manner. To see in this the respective reactions to the new establishment of the rabbinate in Jabne has much it commend itself, but it is unprovable as long as we cannot say what significance Jabne had in this phase of history, whether Josephus even knew about Jabne, or to what degree the teachers of Jabne had dealings with the first Christian communities and how converted Christians reacted to this.

The main problem in the investigation of the continuum from Pharisees to Rabbis is rabbinic literature. The early texts barely document the rabbinic heritage; in fact, they appear rather to conceal it. This makes the investigation of a continuum bridging the year 70 C.E. especially difficult. Names, of course, are not everything. Teachers and ideas are an essential point of comparison. The significance of tradition alongside the written Torah, of a belief in the resurrection, and of efforts for certain regulations regarding ritual purity and taxes characterize the Pharisees in Josephus and the New Testament, but they dominate in the rabbinic tradition.[211] But are these few points enough to permit us to speak of a Pharisaic stamp on the character of the rabbinate, particularly when we are unable to demonstrate a direct continuity with *halakic* parallels (see p. 83f.)?

The Mishnah plays a special role as the basic document of rabbinic Judaism. Is the Mishnah a continuation of Pharisaic themes and interests? As J. Neusner has demonstrated, only a few of the laws in the Mishnah predate the period before 70 C.E. Only the regulations regarding ritual purity form a closed system before 70.[212] In addition, Neusner believes that regulations concerning meals and marriage present additional difficulties. Because of Gamaliel and Simeon ben Gamaliel, whom other sources designate as Pharisees and who are also very important in the Mishnah, we usually assume

211. S. J. D. Cohen, *The Significance,* 38, states with appropriate reservation, "In all likelihood there was some close connection between the post-70 rabbis and the pre-70 rabbis."

212. For this, see J. Neusner, *The Mishnah before 70* (Atlanta, 1987).

"that the Mishnah is a Pharisaic book. While this may well be so, the internal evidence of the Mishnah itself does not direct our attention only to the Pharisees."[213] The line of continuity back to priestly writings is especially important and with it the interconnection of priesthood and Temple. Behind these laws there is perhaps something like "a cultic sect, a holiness order, expressing the aspirations of lay people to live as if they belonged to the caste of priests, and of priests to live as if the whole country were the Temple."[214]

The priestly element in the Mishnah is certainly much stronger than what we would expect to come from Pharisees. The Pharisaic interest in regulations regarding cleanliness is attested for the period before 70 c.e. only by Mark 7 (and parallels), where, however, we are occasionally reminded of a later transference of the controversy from the Sadducees to the Pharisees. Even if we do not want to go so far, the theme of cleanliness (a total of a third of the Mishnah) is, in any case, primarily a priestly concern. The same is true of marital laws, which the priests especially had to observe, and of laws regarding food (especially regarding the priestly offering). This would suggest that after 70 c.e. the priests must have had a special interest in continuing their traditions and laws, leading up to a reconstruction of the Temple, which they would carry over into secular everyday life. Maintaining the offering for the priests even during a period when there was no longer a temple also points in this direction. The role of the high priest Simon the Righteous in the chain of tradition of *m.* ʾ*Abot* also argues in favor of the idea of priestly interests.

We could, of course, interpret all of this as a Pharisaic offer to make a compromise. In order that we might counteract an overemphasis on the priestly element, we might remind ourselves that even before 70 the Pharisees had transferred certain priestly concepts into the everyday life of the average Israelite, thus devaluing the privileged position of the priests (evidence for this is difficult to

213. J. Neusner, *Judaism,* 70.
214. J. Neusner, *Judaism,* 119. He suggests that the beginnings of the ideas of the Mishnah were formed by radical priests, who then added lay people to their company in order to form a "holiness sect" (50).

produce). Rabbinic texts about the controversies with the Sadducees on matters of ritual purity, as in cultic matters, could also point in this direction—as does the lack of high priests in the genealogy of the rabbis (with the exception of the Simon the Righteous) from the period before 70.

Certainly, in the rabbinic texts there are points of contact with concepts that we recognize as Pharisaic, yet these are not *exclusively* Pharisaic. Even the scribal element in the rabbinic texts is not exclusively a Pharisaic heritage. Already during the rebellion against Rome the boundaries between the various Jewish schools lost their significance. Likewise, the new beginning in Jabne is probably not to be interpreted as an exclusive triumph of the Pharisaic groups that remained, but rather as a consciously combined movement that garnered the most diverse branches of Judaism in the interest of national unity.[215] Johanan ben Zakkai, as the founder of the school of Jabne, is never designated as a Pharisee. In *m. Yad.* 4.6 he appears to distance himself much more from the Pharisees. Only later is he replaced by Gamaliel, whom the rabbinic literature labels a Pharisee, but no more so than any other rabbi.

If priestly concerns are so strongly represented at the beginning of the Mishnaic tradition, during the course of time they recede in importance (thus, with the exception of Niddah, there is no gemara to the laws regarding ritual purity, but there is also no Palestinian gemara to the order of Qodashim with its laws about the Temple and sacrifice). This might indicate a shift in the composition of the rabbinic movement, when there was still hope for a speedy rebuilding of the Temple. Perhaps the priestly circle still played a greater role in Jabne than we usually suppose, and only in the course of time were they displaced by Pharisaic and other groups. The rabbinic narrative of the temporary replacement of Gamaliel by the

215. Thus S. J. D. Cohen, *The Significance,* 45, who regards Jabne as determined by an ideology of pluralism. "As a result of this effort to minimize sectarian self-identification, the rabbis did not see themselves as Pharisees and showed little interest in their sectarian roots" (49); Jabne was "a grand coalition of different groups and parties" (50).

high priest Eleazar ben Azariah[216] is probably to be interpreted as a reference to leadership struggles in the new movement.

If we may be permitted to regard the rabbis as a combined movement, the immediate leadership role of the former Pharisees is not so certain. This would mean from the outset that we might locate the Pharisaic heritage in rabbinic writings, but the rabbinic statements that are not attested before 70 c.e. cannot be used directly to supplement our portrait of the Pharisees.[217]

The examination of the sources and especially the fact that only one element of the tradition of the Mishnah even mentions the Pharisees demonstrate that we cannot place the early rabbis in a neat continuum with the Pharisees. Simply to conclude from this that the name *Pharisee* was not a self-designation of the school but something that goes back to their enemies would be a premature weakening of the question of continuity. However, the texts do not justify the view of A. Guttmann, that after 70 c.e. the progressive wing of the Pharisees won out, while the reactionary Pharisaic marginal groups did not accept necessary changes and were disparagingly called "Pharisees" by the rabbis.[218]

Whether the genealogy claimed by the rabbis in *m. ʾAbot* should be regarded as exclusively Pharisaic[219] is likewise debatable. The

<hr />

216. For this, see R. Goldenberg, "The Deposition of Rabban Gamaliel II: An Examination of the Sources," *JJS* 23 (1972): 167-90.

217. J. Lightstone, *Sadducees,* 217: "It does not appear that the road back to the nature of the pre-70 controversy between the Sadducees and the Pharisees is through rabbinic literature."

218. A. Guttmann, *Pharisaism,* 207ff.: since the rabbis condemned the Pharisees of their own time, insofar as they were able, they avoided calling their venerable predecessors from the period of the Temple Pharisees. Similarly, J. Bowker, *Jesus,* 41ff., who regards the "Pharisees" in the decades before 70 c.e. as the extreme wing of the wider movement—the ®akamim; he would connect them with the *Perušim* of the rabbinic texts and the Pharisees in Josephus with the rabbinic ®akamim.

219. J. Neusner, *The Pharisees,* 1:61, for example, speaks without additional support of "the Avot and Hagigah chains of *Pharisaic* tradition" (emphasis mine, but see also n. 43). Frequently *ʾAbot* 1 is seen as a Pharisaic document. Thus, for example, A. I. Baumgarten, *The Pharisaic Paradosis,* 67, n. 16: "old Pharisaic

amplifications by Johanan ben Zacchai and Gamaliel at the end of the chapter might argue in favor of the idea that *m. ʾAbot* 1 was a reworking of an older document,[220] but because of internecine rabbinic conflicts this genealogy might likewise have been produced at a still later time. The proverbial wisdom of *ʾAbot* is thus also not to be regarded as a mark of specific Pharisaic piety. Already the statement ascribed to Hillel should warn us against that: "Do not separate yourselves (*ʾal tiproš*) from the community" (2.4).

The commonly held belief that the *Scroll of Fasts* is supposed to have been a Pharisaic text that was adopted by the rabbis is likewise problematic. The argument that it contains a whole series of anti-Sadducean feast days[221] is supported only by Talmudic texts and the medieval scholium, which are quite far removed from the period in which the *Scroll of Fasts* originated and which probably have no authentic information about the real bases of the specific dates. If we assume that in Jabne as broad a basis as possible was sought, the commemoration of the victories over other branches of Judaism would not have been the best way to produce the desired unity.

We have observed that in later rabbinic texts the Pharisees are more important and are occasionally equated with the "wise ones" (thus, for example, in *b. Qidd.* 66a). A. J. Avery-Peck suggests that the rabbis were, at the outset, hardly asserting that they were continuing the Pharisaic tradition. Only as the rabbis grew in strength "did rabbinic authorities dare to rewrite their own history and to claim as their ancestors the Pharisaic group, remembered for its power and piety."[222] This increasing reflection on the Pharisees,

document at the core of the first chapter of m. ʾAbot," citing M. D. Herr, "Continuum in the Chain of Torah Transmission" (Hebrew), *Zion* 44 (1979): 43-56. Thus far there is no convincing argument.

220. See A. J. Saldarini, "The End of the Rabbinic Chain of Tradition," *JBL* 93 (1974): 97–106.

221. H. Lichtenstein, "Die Fastenrolle: Eine Untersuchung zur Jüdisch-Hellenistischen Geschichte," *HUCA* 8–9 (1931f.): 257–351, 290–98.

222. A. J. Avery-Peck, *The Mishnaic Division of Agriculture,* 361.

remarkably right in the Babylonian Talmud,[223] causes us to ask what knowledge and what traditions underlie this increased Pharisaization of their own history. Here, as in many of the points of the history and influence of the religious schools of Judaism, there are more questions than answers.

223. S. J. D. Cohen, *The Significance*, 39: "The amoraim, especially the amoraim of Babylonia, begin to see themselves more clearly as the descendents of the Pharisees."

GLOSSARY

ʾAbot. 'Fathers,' a tractate of the Mishnah. It combines a genealogy of the rabbinic movement with religious proverbial wisdom.

ʿAm ha-ʾareṣ. 'People of the land,' the population of the country who do not observe religious regulations (especially in matters of tithing and ritual purity) or are untrained in matters of religion.

Baraita. 'External,' in other words, a teaching that is not contained in the Mishnah but is supposed to have come from the time of the Mishnah.

Boethusian. Group in Judaism that is related to or equivalent to the Sadducees. It was probably established by Herod and named for the high priestly family of Boethos.

®aber. 'Comrade,' member of a religious society (*ḥabura*) that is concerned with special precision, especially in matters of tithing and ritual purity.

Ḥasidim. See Hasidean.

ʿErub. 'Mixing,' joining of several private and/or public areas into a single private area in which doing certain things is also permitted on the Sabbath.

Etrog. 'Citron,' a citrus fruit, part of the festal bouquet at the Feast of Tabernacles.

Gemara. 'Completion,' interpretation of the Mishnah in the Talmud.

Halakah. Religious law or the totality of these laws, especially as set down in the Mishnah, thus also an extract from the Mishnah.

Hasidean. 'Pious one,' a branch of Judaism at the time of the Maccabean revolt, mentioned in the books of the Maccabees, often regarded as the parent movement of the Pharisees and the Essenes.

Megillat Taanit. 'Scroll of Fasts,' Aramaic list of days on which it was not permitted to fast on account of the joyful events of the past. The document (second century) was amplified by a Hebrew commentary (scholium) during the Middle Ages.

Mekhilta. Early rabbinic commentary on Exodus (third century?).

Menorah. Seven-branched lamp in the Temple.

Mezuzah. A container at a door containing Bible texts.

Mishnah. '(Oral) teaching,' a corpus of doctrine, circa 200 C.E., edited by Jehuda ha-Nasi, the basis of the Talmud.

Scroll of Fasts. See Megillat Taanit.

Sifra. Early rabbinic commentary on Leviticus (third century?).

Sifre. Early rabbinic commentaries on Numbers and Deuteronomy (third century?).

Talmud. 'Teaching,' commentary and unfolding of the Mishnah. The Palestinian (Jerusalem) Talmud originated in the fifth century. The Babylonian (or simply the Talmud) was edited in the sixth through seventh centuries.

Tannaite. Teacher from the period of the Mishnah (the "tannaitic period").

Tebul Yom. 'One who is submerged on the same day,' someone who has completed the bath of ritual purification but will be completely clean only at sundown.

Tefillin. 'Prayer strips, or phylacteries,' leather-covered boxes containing biblical passages that are bound to the forehead and arm by leather straps.

Tosepta. 'Amplification,' a work corresponding to the Mishnah and amplifying it, probably from the third century.

Selected Bibliography

Alon, G. "The Attitude of the Pharisees to Roman Rule and the House of Herod." In *Jews, Judaism and the Classical World,* 18–47. Jerusalem, 1977.

Avery-Peck, A. J. *Mishnah's Division of Agriculture: A History and Theology of Seder Seraim.* Chico, Calif., 1985.

Baumbach, G. *Jesus von Nazareth im Lichte der jüdischen Gruppenbildung.* Berlin, 1971.

_____. "Das Sadduzäerverständnis bei Josephus Flavius und im NT." *Kairos* 13 (1971): 17–37.

_____. "Der sadduzäische Konservatismus." In *Literatur und Religion des Frühjudentums,* ed. J. Maier and J. Schreiner, 201–13. Würzburg, 1973.

Baumgarten, A. I. "The Name of the Pharisees." *JBL* 102 (1983): 411–28.

_____. "Josephus and Hippolytus on the Pharisees." *HUCA* 55 (1984): 1–25.

_____. "Korban and the Pharisaic Paradosis." *JANESCU* 16–17 (1984–85 [memorial to E. Bickerman]): 5–17.

_____. "The Pharisaic Paradosis." *HTR* 80 (1987): 63–77.

Baumgarten, J. M. *Studies in Qumran Law.* Leiden, 1977.

_____. "The Pharisaic-Sadducean Controversies about Purity and the Qumran Texts." *JJS* 31 (1980): 157–70.

_____. "Halakhic Polemics in New Fragments from Qumran Cave 4." In *Biblical Archaeology Today,* 390–99. Jerusalem, 1985.

Beall, T. S. *Josephus' Description of the Essenes Illustrated by the Dead Sea Scrolls.* Cambridge, 1988.

Beattie, D. R. G. "The Targum of Ruth—A Sectarian Composition?" *JJS* 36 (1985): 222–29.

Beckwith, R. T. "The Pre-History and Relationship of the Pharisees, Sadducees and Essenes: A Tentative Reconstruction." *RQ* 11 (1982): 3–46.

Berger, K. "Jesus als Pharisäer und frühe Christen als Pharisäer." *NovT* 30 (1988): 231–62.

Bowker, J. W. *Jesus and the Pharisees*. Cambridge, 1973.

Braun, W. "Were the NT Herodians Essenes? A Critique of an Hypothesis." *RQ* 14/53 (1989): 75–88.

Brownlee, W. H. *The Midrash Pesher of Habakkuk*. Missoula, Mont., 1979.

———. "The Wicked Priest, the Man of Lies, and the Righteous Teacher—The Problem of Identity." *JQR* 73 (1982–83): 1–37.

Callaway, P. R. *The History of the Qumran Community: An Investigation*. Sheffield, 1988.

Carroll, J. T. "Luke's Portrayal of the Pharisees." *CBQ* 50 (1988): 604–21.

Charlesworth, J. H. "The Origin and Subsequent History of the Authors of the Dead Sea Scrolls: Four Transitional Phases among the Qumran Essenes." *RQ* 10 (1979–81): 213–33.

Cohen, S. J. D. *Josephus in Galilee and Rome*. Leiden, 1979.

———. "The Significance of Yavneh: Pharisees, Rabbis, and the End of Jewish Sectarianism." *HUCA* 55 (1984): 27–53.

Daniel, C. "Les 'Hérodiens' du Nouveau Testament sont-ils des Esséniens?" *RQ* 6 (1967–69): 31–53.

———. "Les Esséniens et 'ceux qui sont dans les maisons des rois' (Matthieu 11, 7–8 et Luc 7, 24–25)." *RQ* 6 (1967–69): 261–77.

———. "'Faux Prophètes': surnom des Esséniens dans le Sermon sur la Montagne." *RQ* 7 (1969–71): 45–79.

———. "Nouveaux arguments en faveur de l'identification des Hérodiens et des Esséniens." *RQ* 7 (1969–71): 397–402.

Davies, P. "Hasidism in the Maccabean Period." *JJS* 28 (1977): 127–40.

Efron, J. *Studies on the Hasmonean Period*. Leiden, 1987.

Feldman, L. "The Identity of Pollio, the Pharisee, in Josephus." *JQR* 49 (1958): 53–62.

Finkel, A. *The Pharisees and the Teacher of Nazareth.* Leiden-Cologne, 1964.

Finkelstein, L. *The Pharisees: The Sociological Background of Their Faith,* 2 vols. 3rd ed. Philadelphia, 1962.

Flusser, D. "Pharisäer, Sadduzäer und Essener im Pescher Nahum." In *Qumran,* ed. K. E. Grözinger et al., 121–66. Darmstadt, 1981.

García Martínez, F. "Orígenes del movimiento esenio y orígenes qumránicos: Pistas para una solución." *Simposio bíblico español* (Córdoba, 1985), 527–56. Valencia-Córdoba, 1987.

Geller, M. J. "Alexander Jannaeus and the Pharisee Rift." *JJS* 30 (1979): 202–11.

Goldstein, J. A. *I Maccabees.* AB 41. Garden City, N.Y., 1976.

Goodblatt, D. "The Place of the Pharisees in First Century Judaism: The State of the Debate." *JSJ* 20 (1989): 12–30.

Goodman, M. *The Ruling Class of Judaea: The Origins of the Jewish Revolt against Rome 66–70.* Cambridge, 1987.

Guttmann, A. "Pharisaism in Transition." In *Studies in Rabbinic Judaism,* 206–23. New York, 1976.

Hann, R. R. "The Community of the Pious: The Social Setting of the Psalms of Solomon." *SR* 17 (1988): 169–89.

Hengel, M. *Judentum und Hellenismus.* 2nd ed. Tübingen, 1973.

————. *Die Zeloten.* Leiden, 1961.

Herr, M. D. "Who Were the Boethusians?" (Hebrew). *Seventh World Congress of Jewish Studies, Studies in the Talmud, Halacha and Midrash,* 1–20. Jerusalem, 1981.

Hoehner, H. W. *Herod Antipas.* Cambridge, 1972.

Horgan, M. P. *Pesharim: Qumran Interpretations of Biblical Books.* Washington, 1979.

Hummel, R. *Die Auseinandersetzung zwischen Kirche und Judentum in Matthäusevangelium.* 2nd ed. Munich, 1966.

Hunzinger, C.-H. "Spuren pharisäischer Institutionen in der frühen rabbinischen Überlieferung." In *Tradition und Glaube,* FS K. G. Kuhn, ed. G. Jeremias, H. W. Kuhn, and H. Stegemann, 147–56. Göttingen, 1971.

Isenberg, S. "An Anti-Sadducee Polemic in the Palestinian Targumic Tradition." *HTR* 63 (1970): 433–44.

Jeremias, J. *Jerusalem zur Zeit Jesu.* 2nd ed. Göttingen, 1958.

Kampen, J. *The Hasideans and the Origin of Pharisaism: A Study in 1 and 2 Maccabees.* Atlanta, 1988.

Katz, S. T. "Issues in the Separation of Judaism and Christianity after 70 C.E.: A Reconsideration." *JBL* 103 (1984): 43–76.

Kieval, P. "The Talmudic View of the Hasmonean and Early Herodian Periods in Jewish History." Diss., Brandeis, 1970.

Kilgallen, J. J. "The Sadducees and Resurrection from the Dead: Luke 20, 27–40." *Bib* 67 (1986): 478–95.

Kister, M. "Concerning the History of the Essenes—A Study of the Animal Apocalypse, The Book of Jubilees and the Damascus Covenant" (Hebrew). *Tarbiz* 56 (1986–87): 1–18.

Lachs, S. T. "The Pharisees and the Sadducees on Angels: Acts XXIII.8." *Gratz College Annual of Jewish Studies* 6 (1977): 35–42.

_____. "Why Was the 'Amen' Response Interdicted in the Temple?" *JSJ* 19 (1988): 230–40.

Le Moyne, J. *Les Sadducéens.* Paris, 1972.

Levine, L. I. "On the Political Involvement of the Pharisees under Herod and the Procurators" (Hebrew). *Cathedra* 8 (1978): 16–20.

_____. *The Political Struggle between Pharisees and Sadducees in the Hasmonean Period* (Hebrew) (memorial to A. Schalit), 61–68. Jerusalem, 1980.

Lieu, J. M. "Epiphanius on the Scribes and Pharisees (Pan. 15.1–16.4)." *JTS* 39 (1988): 509–24.

Lightstone, J. "Sadducees versus Pharisees: The Tannaitic Sources." In *Christianity, Judaism and Other Greco-Roman Cults: Studies for M. Smith,* ed. J. Neusner, 206–17. Leiden, 1975.

Lührmann, D. "Die Pharisäer und die Schriftgelehrten im Markusevangelium." *ZNW* 78 (1987): 169–85.

Luz, U. "Jesus und die Pharisäer." *Judaica* 38 (1982): 229–46.

Maier, G. *Mensch und freier Wille nach den jüdischen Religionsparteien zwischen Ben Sira und Paulus.* Tübingen, 1971.

Maier, J. "Weitere Stücke zum Nahumkommentar aus der Höhle 4 von Qumran." *Judaica* 18 (1962): 215–50.

Malik, J. T. "Die Geschichte der Essener." In *Qumran,* ed. K. E. Grözinger et al., 58–120. Darmstadt, 1981.

Mason, S. N. *Flavius Josephus on the Pharisees.* Leiden, 1990. (Not seen.)

————. "Priesthood in Josephus and 'the Pharisaic Revolution.'" *JBL* 107 (1988): 657–61.

————. "Was Josephus a Pharisee? A Re-Examination of Life 10–12." *JJS* 40 (1989): 30–45.

Meyer, R. *Tradition und Neuschöpfung im antiken Judentum: Dargestellt an der Geschichte des Pharisäismus.* Berlin, 1965.

————. S.v. "saddukaios." *TWNT* 7: 35–54.

————. S.v. "pharisaios (Judentum)." *TWNT* 9: 11–36.

Moessner, D. P. "The 'Leaven of the Pharisees' and 'This Generation': Israel's Rejection of Jesus according to Luke." *JSNT* 34 (1988): 21–46.

Moore, G. F. "Schicksal und freier Wille in der jüdischen Philosophie bei Josephus." In *Zur Josephforschung,* ed. A. Schalit, 167–89. Darmstadt, 1973. English original in *HTR* 22 (1929): 371–89.

Mowery, R. L. "Pharisees and Scribes, Galilee and Jerusalem." *ZNW* 80 (1989): 266–68.

Müller, K. "Jesus und die Sadduzäer." In *Biblische Randbemerkungen,* FS R. Schnackenburg, 3–24. Würzburg, 1974.

Murphy-O'Connor, J. "The Essenes and Their History." *RB* 81 (1974): 215–44.

Neusner, J. *The Rabbinic Traditions about the Pharisees before 70,* 3 vols. Leiden, 1971.

————. *From Politics to Piety: The Emergence of Pharisaic Judaism.* Englewood Cliffs, N.J., 1973.

————. "The Written Tradition in the Pre-Rabbinic Period." *JSJ* 4 (1973): 76–85.

————. *Judaism: The Evidence of the Mishnah.* Chicago, 1981.

————. "The Pharisees: Rabbinic Perspectives." In *Studies in Ancient Judaism.* Hoboken, 1985.

_____. "Josephus' Pharisees: A Complete Repertoire." In *Josephus, Judaism and Christianity,* ed. L. H. Feldman and G. Hata, 274–92. Leiden, 1987. Also published without the introduction as "Josephus' Pharisees" in *Ex Orbe Religionum: Studia Geo Widengren* (Leiden, 1972), 224–44.

Patrich, J. "A Sadducean Halakha and the Jerusalem Aqueduct." *The Jerusalem Cathedra* 2 (1982): 25–39.

Plöger, O. *Theokratie und Eschatologie.* 2nd ed. Neukirchen, 1962.

Qimron, E., and J. Strugnell. "An Unpublished Halakhic Letter from Qumran." In *Biblical Archeology Today,* 400–407. Jerusalem, 1985.

Rivkin, E. *A Hidden Revolution.* Nashville, 1978.

Saldarini, A. J. *Pharisees, Scribes and Sadducees: A Sociological Approach.* Edinburgh, 1989.

Sanders, E. P. *Paul and Palestinian Judaism.* Philadelphia, 1977.

_____. *Jesus and Judaism.* London, 1985.

Sanders, J. T. *The Jews in Luke-Acts.* London, 1987.

Schalit, A. *König Herodes: Der Mann und sein Werk.* Berlin, 1969.

Schiffman, L. H. *The Halakhah at Qumran.* Leiden, 1975.

Schnelle, U. "Jesus, ein Jude aus Galiläa." *BZ* 32 (1988): 107–13.

Schubert, K. *Die jüdischen Religionsparteien in neutestamentlicher Zeit.* Stuttgart, 1970.

Schürer, E. *The History of the Jewish People in the Age of Jesus Christ (175 B.C.–A.D. 135),* 3 vols. Revised and edited by G. Vermes and F. Millar. Edinburgh, 1973–87.

Schwankl, O. *Die Sadduzäerfrage (Mk 12, 18–27 parr).* Bonn, 1987.

Schwartz, D. R. "Josephus and Nicolaus on the Pharisees." *JSJ* 14 (1983): 157–71.

_____. "'Scribes and Pharisees, Hypocrites': Who were the Scribes?" (Hebrew). *Zion* 50 (1985): 121–32.

Smith, M. "Palestinian Judaism in the First Century." In *Israel: Its Role in Civilization,* ed. M. Davis, 67–81. New York, 1956.

Spiro, S. J. "Who was the ®aber? A New Approach to an Ancient Institution." *JSJ* 11 (1980): 186–216.

Tscherikover, V. *Hellenistic Civilization and the Jews.* Philadelphia, 1959.

Thoma, C. "Der Pharisäismus." In *Literatur und Religion des Früh-judentums,* ed. J. Maier and J. Schreiner, 254–72. Würzburg, 1973.

Van der Woude, A. S. "Wicked Priest or Wicked Priests?" *JJS* 33 (1982 [FS Y. Yadin]): 349–59.

Vermes, G. *The Dead Sea Scrolls: Qumran in Perspective.* London, 1982.

Wächter, L. "Die unterschiedliche Haltung der Pharisäer, Sadduzäer und Essener zur *heimarmene* nach dem Bericht des Josephus." *ZRGG* 21 (1969): 97–114.

Weiss, H.-F. "Der Pharisäismus im Lichte der Überlieferung des Neuen Testaments." In *Tradition und Neuschöpfung im antiken Judentum,* ed. R. Meyer, 89–132. Berlin, 1965.

_____. S.v. "pharisaios (NT, Frühchristl. Literatur)." *TWNT* 9:36–51.

Whitely, D. E. H. "Was John Written by a Sadducee?" *ANRW* II 25/3, 2481–2505. Berlin-New York, 1985.

Wild, R. A. "The Encounter between Pharisaic and Christian Judaism: Some Early Gospel Evidence." *NovT* 27 (1985): 105–24.

Yadin, Y. *The Temple Scroll,* 3 vols. Jerusalem, 1983.

Ziesler, J. A. "Luke and the Pharisees." *NTS* 25 (1979): 146–57.

INDEXES

157